GAYBULLAEV OTABEK
MUKHAMMADIEVICH

IN THE UZBEK MENTALITY OF GLOBALIZATION IMPACT ON AESTHETIC CULTURE

Monograph

© Gaybullaev Otabek Mukhammadievich
In the Uzbek Mentality of Globalization Impact on Aesthetic Culture
by: Gaybullaev Otabek Mukhammadievich
Edition: November '2024
Publisher:
Taemeer Publications LLC (Michigan, USA / Hyderabad, India)

ISBN 978-93-5872-284-0

© **Gaybullaev Otabek Mukhammadievich**

Book	:	**In the Uzbek Mentality of Globalization Impact on Aesthetic Culture**
Author	:	Gaybullaev Otabek Mukhammadievich
Publisher	:	Taemeer Publications
Year	:	'2024
Pages	:	274
Title Design	:	*Taemeer Web Design*

Samarkand – 2024

In this monograph, a philosophical analysis of ideological processes in the national mentality of the Uzbek people, developed over the centuries, a philosophical study of the issues of the influence of ethnomangular States on a healthy sedentary lifestyle in the development of social life in the management of society. It reflects the views that globalization retains its essence under the influence of the cultural heritage that humanity has created between historical periods, moral laws and regulations, the aesthetic ideal of cultures. The historical significance of language in the development of the Uzbek mentality through aesthetic culture of its modern image, the influence of moral culture on social relations, has been scientifically studied.

The monograph is intended for specialists working in the field of philosophy, aesthetics, ethics, cultural studies, scientific researchers and others interested in the field of social and humanitarian Sciences.

CONTENT

Introduction 6

Chapter One. Ideological, spiritual-ideological and pragmatic essence of aesthetic culture in the Uzbek mentality 13

1.1. Interaction of aesthetic culture with national ideas and ideology in the Uzbek mentality 13

1.2. The influence of aesthetic culture on a healthy lifestyle of ethnomethnic and spiritual-ideological state in the Uzbek mentality 47

1.3. Constructive significance of art in the formation of aesthetic culture in the Uzbek mentality 84

Chapter Two. The peculiarities of the formation of aesthetic culture in the Uzbek mentality in the process of globalization 118

2.1. Distinctive features in the formation of aesthetic culture in the era of globalization 118

2.2. Issues of harmonization of aesthetic culture with valeoesthetic education in the Uzbek mentality 147

2.3. Factors and prospects for raising aesthetic culture in the Uzbek mentality 182

Chapter Three. Language issues in the Uzbek mentality in Central Asia during globalization 210

2.1. The role of national values in increasing the moral culture of youth in the era of globalization ....…....…... 210

2.2. Philosophical foundations of the development of aesthetic culture in society……………………………………………. 225

2.3. Processes of development of linguistic and philosophical views on the land of Central Asia……………………………………….. 240

Conclusion 262

A list of used literature................. ……….. 268

Introduction

Social progress has put the preservation of national values on the agenda as one of the pressing issues, deeply perceiving the philosophical ideas of the young generation, being, among political, social and spiritual reforms in all spheres of society's life. The main goal of the state, aimed at reforms in the spiritual sphere, was to prepare the ground for the moral and aesthetic rise of our people, in particular, to develop a scientifically based educational system in which each person grows up to be humane, patriotic, selfless, passionate people.

The importance of aesthetic thinking and the prosperity of aesthetic culture is great in the growth of personality as educated, responsible, politically perceptive, legally literate, morally pure and spiritually harmonious. Aesthetic education and culture are to some extent molded, without a hardened educational system, and the formation and development of a new aesthetic thinking of young people is of great importance in spiritual reform, since the activity of the individual is a process associated with all types and branches. For this, a huge amount of work has been carried out and is being carried out on the scale of the new Uzbekistan. Because aesthetic thinking and culture are formed, a developed person seeks to widely promote the history, spiritual heritage of his people. Such a person will not be indifferent to today's social progress, will closely connect his life and activities with the development and prospects of the motherland, will not imagine himself outside the nation, country and socio-historical life.

The development of aesthetic culture enhances activity in the individual, encourages to test and realize their creative capabilities. Such a socio-historical and spiritually extremely necessary issue – the study of the formation and development of the aesthetic culture of the individual is an urgent issue, both theoretical and practical. The upbringing of a physically strong, morally pure, aesthetically cultured, spiritually harmonious generation in society is a priority of state policy. If we are referring to the spiritual reforms carried out in our country over the past years, in fact, the upbringing of a healthy generation has risen to the level of Public Policy. The state programs adopted every year provide for the formation and development of a spiritually higher generation, whose personality is not only physically, but also politically, legally, morally, aesthetically and philosophically aligned with national values.

In the era of globalization, the development of the aesthetic culture of the individual plays a huge role in the upbringing and upbringing of a physically healthy mentally-active generation. Zero aesthetic culture practices the individual as a mirror of human spirituality in realizing their attitude and goals towards life. Consequently, in the concept of a healthy generation of our President, aesthetic thinking, development and prosperity of Culture also occupy a special place and gain great scientific importance. In the construction of a future great state in social life, a noble task and responsibility is assigned to a person with a high aesthetic culture and ideal. Raising the aesthetic culture of a person, upbringing is not an easy task. Especially in our time-in a time when ideologies have become more transparent, Goh pinhona, various extremist currents and fanatics are trying to divert weak-willed and thinned young people to their side, this issue becomes extremely relevant. Therefore, in order to realize and develop the feelings of creativity of the individual, it will be necessary, first of all, to enjoy them with the noble traditions of our people, purma'no oghits and educational traditions, to arm themselves with socio-philosophical, human ideas that unite history and today's era.

The most basic function of aesthetic culture in society is to protect the individual from foreign influences, to teach him to live life with pleasure, to achieve spiritual and spiritual perfection, which is an example for others and brings the air of others. The involvement of the individual, in particular young people, in the socio-economic and spiritual spheres, in the work being done in the path of the need of members of society, further increasing their activity, has become one of the main tasks of state policy. The absorption of the philosophical and aesthetic essence of such reforms taking place in the socio-political life of our country into the consciousness, thinking and culture of the individual, their upbringing in the spirit of a national idea became a requirement of the period. Because individuals who are the founders of democratic and civil society are embodied as active subjects in social life, living and functioning under the laws of beauty.

The serious conduct of youth education in

every branch of the educational system, in particular, the determination of the content of national and universal moral and aesthetic values in the minds of each individual, the study of the issue of the formation and development of their aesthetic culture on the basis of the demand of the time, is an urgent scientific problem today. Changes, innovations, reforms taking place in the new Uzbekistan will not affect the life of young people either. Therefore, it is necessary for young people to realize the events and phenomena occurring in social life teran on the basis of the requirements of national ideology, aesthetic culture and, based on this, realize their mental and physical abilities, spiritual capabilities. In young people, it is difficult to achieve the goals pursued without the formation of such skills, knowledge and moral perfection. Therefore, in determining the spiritual image of young people, the study of the formation and development of aesthetic culture, a factor that plays an important role in their formation as a socially active person, has an important socio – philosophical significance.

The integration of Uzbekistan into the international community as an equal subject of international law, changes taking place in the field of Science and technology, economic relations, updates in the process of building civil society put the issue of studying socio-philosophical issues of the rise of aesthetic thinking of citizens of New Uzbekistan, researching the laws and categories of aesthetics in a state In the process of developing the aesthetics of living in society on the basis of a combination of national and universal values, great attention is paid to the principle of humanism.

The issue of maturing the moral and aesthetic consciousness, worldview, thinking, culture, spirituality of the individual has attracted the attention of thinkers, philosophers, aesthetic scientists, psychics and creators as the most pressing scientific-theoretical and practical problem at all stages of human development.

Acquaintance with the philosophical, aesthetic and pedagogical-psychological literature and Research created in the following years shows that scientific works and articles dedicated to aesthetic culture and aesthetic education are developing in a modern way on a national scale. Taking into account this, research is being carried out on the issues of developing a new aesthetic culture of the individual in the following years in this monograph. By developing the aesthetic culture of young people in society, it is the main goal to educate them in the spirit of national and universal spiritual and moral and aesthetic values, to reveal the socio-philosophical essence of adulthood as a healthy and harmonious, socially and creatively active person.

Chapter One. Ideological, spiritual-ideological and pragmatic essence of aesthetic culture in the Uzbek mentality

1.1§. Interaction of aesthetic culture with national ideas and ideology in the Uzbek mentality

The process of social development brings up individuals with a unique and appropriate modern thinking for each period, providing an impetus for the development of society on the basis of a new worldview. In this process, the role of aesthetic culture is strong in the philosophical worldview system, which brings the prospect of the people to a high peak, and a national ideology is formed that takes on a special appearance in the path of the fate of the nation, prosperity of the motherland, peace of the land, prosperity of the people. As its driving force, the main role is played by social relations between the individual and the state, an approach to reality from an aesthetic point of view, a call for people to an aesthetic culture.

Starting from the early days of civil society being established in Uzbekistan, the issue of the formation of nationalism, the creation of a national ideology began to find its bright expression in the system of social relations. "In the field of ideology, what is called emptiness will not be in itself,[1]" sh.M.Mirziyoev, - because the soul, Brain, Mind and thinking of a person never ceases to receive information, to think, to be affected. So he always needs spiritual food. If the same food is not obtained from the environment in which it lives, or if this environment does not satisfy it,what will happen, say? He is slowly looking for such food from the other side. We should not give way to this. Here's what it's about! For this, people who consider themselves responsible for the spirituality of our society, youth, ideological and ideological education-whether it is a neighborhood or religious organizations, law enforcement officers or creative intellectuals with great power of influence – should all be especially active." In such a context, each of us felt the need for a grandiose idea aimed at forming the national feelings of the individual in society, serving, doing for the individual and society, raising the fate of our people to the level of a high aesthetic culture.

---

[1] Mirziyoev Sh. Continuing our path to national development with determination, we will take it to a new level. - T.: Uzbekistan, Volume 1, 2018. P. 484.

As a result, the prosperity of society and the product of striving to exalt the aesthetic culture of the individual, which embodied the long-standing aspirations of our people, led to the emergence of the need for national ideology and its importance at the level of Public Policy. The fact that this issue is extremely relevant is emphasized by the head of the country, who noted that "loyalty naturally leads to lagging behind today's Times, which are developing rapidly, and this is absolutely impossible. That is why political parties, having revised their programmatic goals and objectives, their work in the ideological sphere, make the necessary amendments and additions to them, in which the study of the world experience , strengthening international cooperation, will not be unprofitable.[2]"

On the basis of this ideology, it is relevant to prioritize the interests of the individual in the civil society being built in the new Uzbekistan, to strengthen the state's activities in the process of reform in the interests of the human being. According to the laws of Social Development, the idea and ideology and culture of the individual are

---

[2] Mirziyoev Sh. By persistently continuing our path to national development, we will take it to a new level. - T.: Uzbekistan, Volume 1, 2018. P. 555.

decisive in society. It is in this activity that the need of society for citizens with high tastes increases. This, in turn, requires a strong formation of a certain idea or ideology in all areas of social life, directing people who are becoming the driving force of society towards noble goals. The result is an ideology consisting of a certain set of views and thoughts that reflect the lifestyle of the people, educate a healthy person or the younger generation. This ideology always serves as a power divider for spiritual and spiritual processes, calling people to high heights on the basis of aesthetic ideals. Therefore, " any person, naturally, cannot live without purpose. Consequently, as long as life exists, as long as there are countries, states and their interests, they seek to define their path of development, the horizons of tomorrow through their national idea, national ideology.[3]"

In our society, ideology always serves with its relevance to the formation of folk beliefs, a high aesthetic culture of the individual. Because this ideology serves to express in itself the aesthetic worldview of more than 130 nations and

---

[3] Free and prosperous homeland, free and prosperous life-our ultimate goal. - T.: Volume 8, Uzbekistan, 2000. P. 490.

elates living in Uzbekistan, oriented towards goodness, their spiritual rise in the new century. In our aspirations to build a free and prosperous homeland, a free and prosperous life, which is our ultimate goal to achieve this goal, a source of spiritual and spiritual strength for us, a scientific basis is a national idea, a national ideology. Today, there are many different opinions about the content and essence of the concept of national ideology. The main philosophical roots of national ideology are formed by universal values in World Philosophy, Eastern philosophy and the philosophical views of our allomas grown from our country.

By national ideology, it is necessary to understand the complex of ideas that vividly reflect the material and spiritual needs, principles, goals, interests and aspirations of each nation living in a certain territory. This is a national ideology, interpreting the essence of the national ideology on the basis of his secular ideas by our first president Islam Karimov... is the immortal belief of the people that the nation does not burn in the fire, does not sink in the water[4]".

---

[4] Karimov I.A. I believe in the strong will of our wise people. "The devotee", June 8, 2000.

The national ideology, which matures the goals of the people on the basis of a strong belief, watered with the light of goodness for the prosperity of society, has always nurtured a person who plunges towards new heights and aesthetic cultures.

The national ideology of each individual and nation has not expressed the ideas of one ERA in itself, but manifested itself in the material and spiritual heritage that has been formed in the worldview of humans for thousands of years and passed down from ancestors to generations. In particular, the national ideology of the Uzbek people also developed the worldview of individuals in social life long before the creation of the "Avesto". This is how the basis of his national ideology was Shirak, a person who fought for the freedom of his homeland. When he condemned himself to death in order to preserve the freedom of his people, the peace of the land and his high aesthetic culture, he certainly relied on his national ideology. Because this ideology of his was a mature person who encouraged members of the people to work aimed at the highest good and creative, and encouraged them to make any heroics for a society of high aesthetic culture, and, moreover, for the people to live comfortably, live happily healthy lives.

Great heroes of our homeland, such as Spitamen, Temur Malik, Jaloliddin Manguberdi, named as the Sultan of the largest statesmen and poets, Amir Temur and Mirzo Babur, the sun of our nation – Alisher Navoi also highly appreciated the national ideology in their multifaceted activities, state policy towards different nationalities and elates, and in their works.

Historically, it is known that the Greek invaders, no matter how they tried to subjugate Spetamen, could not achieve this and finally, in the most disgusting way, nomardically managed to kill him. Despite being a simple loser, Spetamen saw the liberation of the peoples of all Central Asia as preferable to any personal wealth and positions, and fought for national pride.

The true love between Timur Malik and Niginabeka, the Tajik daughter of Voruh, the fact that they passed the marriage is a vivid example of how strong veins existed in the hearts of our people in relation to their idea and ideology, even in the past, when this beautiful dancer decided to use the jewels he collected for a lifetime against the Mughal invaders. The fact that jalaliddin Manguberdi also sacrificed his children and fought against the Mughal invaders for a lifetime is a proof not found in human history.

Thanks to the fact that our grandparent really implemented his slogan "Power is justice", he managed to unite all nationalities and nationalities in the territory of Central Asia, establish their relations according to the content of national ideology, build such a great kingdom for the first time in the history of our motherland, and carry out tremendous creative work.

It is known that Emir Temür, as he pointed out in his"Temür traps", followed 12 Rules in conquering States, governing the state and granting it zebu-ornaments. On the tenth of these 12 Rules, Amir Temur paid homage to all the tribes and elates in his refuge. He urged them to follow a national ideology regardless of their nationality. A clear example of this is the fact that, thanks to the implementation of the policy of our great-grandfather, the inhabitants of Movaraunnahr live in grace and harmony of different tribes, people of different nationalities and nationalities: Turks, Arabs, marves, Armenian Christians, Greek Catholics, Jacobians, fire-burning Christians and others. In this famous work, our great ancestor expressed the equality and noble attitude of all nations and elates in society and their place with his thoughts, namely: "the religion of the inhabitants of each country and city, regardless of the urf, I was held in Ashna with the glory and buzzards of the surroundings", "I strengthened my kingdom on the basis of Islam, Torah and salt,"

"Well known to you, our state is a multinational and multi-confessional state. Today, representatives of more than 130 nationalities and nationalities live in our country as children of the same family and cow. In this regard, tolerance, which has long been characteristic of our people, undoubtedly, plays an important role. As a confirmation of this fact, I would like to give an example. The mausoleum, named after the prophet Daniel, was built in the city of Samarkand during the reign of the Holy Prophet Amir Temur, is equally revered by representatives of Islam, Christianity and Judaism[5]".

One of the main reasons for the collapse of the great kingdom established by Amir Temur

---

[5] Mirziyoev Sh. Continuing our path to national development with determination, we will take it to a new level. - T.: Uzbekistan, Volume 1, 2018. P. 464.

was that the place and position of the national ideology, in general, the National idea, in society, fell to a low level. It can be said that on one account, therefore, most of the great structures erected by our great-grandfather Amir Temur bunyod, the pride and honor of benazir of our people, were demolished by Abdullah Khan, of about a hundred buildings built by Ulughbek, only one madrasa survived, most of the buildings founded by Babur were destroyed.

Alisher Navoi also understood the national ideology in a very broad sense and discovered its extremely important aspects. In the opinion of this glorious poet, God's love for human beings is infinite. It is necessary that a person, in response to God's infinite blessing on him, loves all his servants. Only then will the love of all God have expressed and fulfilled his devotion. In other words, loving God begins with loving ordinary people.

Alisher Navoi, in his epic" Saddi Iskandariy", tried to create an artistic image of the vision of the most high-ranking folk Tsar, which for thousands of years has been done in the minds and hearts of our people, personally in his own homes. In this work of His Majesty, Ayni stated that this imaginary King would carry out a national ideology in society, which he remained faithful to this goal for the rest of his life. For example, Alexander not only puts an end to all the injustices that have occurred during his father's reign, eliminates vices, but at the same time treats the peoples of other lands with dishonesty and justice, with compassion and mercy, saves them from the oppression of tyrants and various horrors, fights for Prosperity and prosperity. In particular, Alexander will build a high wall blocking the path of the Yajuj and the Magyjuj, the personification of the archenemy of the peoples living at the foot of Mount Qof. This wall was a wall of justice and tranquility. In its construction, the peoples of different countries, including. Romans, mavoraunnahrites, Persians, Chinese, Indians, Russians, French and other peoples participate.

What kind of work Alisher Navoi does not receive, in which the spiritual and moral vices of a person are condemned, and at the same time, his higher qualities are supported.

During the Soviet era, national ideology was replaced by the concept of internationalism, and interethnic relations were explained in terms of "Soviet people" and "communist ideology", based on the interests of the dominant nation. The unity and harmony of all nations and elates in this state was called the "Soviet people", and there was no national meaning (unsuri) in its content. That is why representatives of more than a hundred nationalities and nationalities living in our homeland have not been brought up in the spirit of real national ideology for more than 70 years. The negative consequences of this are still manifested in the cultural and spiritual life of our society.

It is known that the former Soviet state was victorious over fascist Germany, at the expense of the extremely large number of citizens, the "harsh" handedness of the Soviet leadership, people's hatred of the Nazis and other factors. One of the biggest mistakes made by the German fascists was that they openly declared that all nations and elates of the world were secondary (indigenous) peoples and most of them needed to be destroyed and the rest became slaves of the Germans. It is planned to exterminate the indigenous peoples of Central Asia, including Uzbekistan, and move the Fergana Valley. It is noteworthy that so many similar plans were also laid out in his "will" by Alexander Macedonsky in his time.

We should proudly note that now in our country the national ideology is supported by our state, laws and regulations are being adopted that are necessary for full-fledged operation in all aspects of our social life, etc.

The main goal of the national ideology in our society is to bring citizens to the realization of the goals and objectives set by a mature person of high morale, in all respects harmony, to educate them in intellectual maturity and as a progressive national mentality. Therefore, there is always a national ideology, primacy, the feelings of understanding our own, our sacred traditions, the cherished dreams that have formed our people for many centuries, the higher goals and tasks set before society. Because this ideology encourages the individual to have an aesthetic perception of the beauty of nature, the need for society and the hopes of the nation's dreams.

National ideology encourages each individual to be able to distinguish, appreciate and deeply understand the beauty of national value and lifestyle, to form the ability to distinguish their own nationality from the aesthetic culture of the peoples of the world, to enrich spiritual and social life with the rules of elegance.

Such a spiritual and social process directly serves the rise of the aesthetic culture and thinking of the individual, leading to an increase in their knowledge and skills about morality, decency, history, art, literature, technology, cultural heritage, traditions, religious beliefs. Such aesthetic thinking of a person, harmonized with humanism, democratic principles, national ideology, cannot bend his will even at the moment when tragedies occur, when material difficulties are experiencing days, but also serves to take a personal step towards a bright perspective to build a fair life.

Since the formation and development of the aesthetic culture of the individual is directly related to the establishment of a fair, civil society, the meaning does not come from this to deny the national mentality of other nationalities and peoples living in Uzbekistan. Because it is natural for the formation of its national mentality in young people who are engaged in activities to establish a just civil society that honors the sides of universal values.

Independence also makes the formation and

development of interaction and common aspects of such national mentalities an objective necessity. Regardless of the nationality, religion and race of the person living in Uzbekistan, they are united by universal aesthetic values, national ideology and ideals of building a just society.

President Sh.M.As Mirziyoev noted, " it is extremely important to prepare a new generation of personnel, a new class of investors, who will effectively use innovation and investments, forming the state's innovation renewal program. This requires a strong national idea, a national program for the technological development of Uzbekistan and the modernization of the domestic market. This program should make it possible to bring Uzbekistan to the world's progressive countries more quickly.[6] "

The general object of national ideology is a person, and in his conscious, intelligent, perceptual actions, aesthetic ideals, processions, lifestyle, treatment, morality, manners, traditions, the national mentality finds its expression. Such a socio-spiritual process, in turn, the fact that every younger generation should be honored as a person

---
[6] Mirziyoev Sh.M. The consent of our people is the highest grade given to our activities. - T.: Uzbekistan, Volume 2, 2018. P. 116.

regardless of nationality, race, lineage, religion, faith is the main criterion of a fair system. Because a just social life is a spiritual need that humanity dreams of, not just for a nation or country without belonging.

It is the main task of the national ideology to encourage such a person to associate the fate of the nation with the fate of the nation, the fate of the nation with the fate of the universal, and to educate and bring up such young people. "the rich cultural and spiritual heritage of our people, passing through the trials of Moses, national values, traditions and traditions, the spirit of freedom in holidays and ceremonies, the spirit of the struggle for freedom, the courage shown by our ancestors in the path of independence, the work of creativity and the way of thinking that spiritual spirit gave them in their implementation. It has stood the test of years for centuries, polished and improved.[7]" Therefore, in a country where a new national ideology is formed and stable, a new aesthetic culture of the individual, his attitude to Universal intellectual values, is

---

[7] Khojanova T.J. Ideological prevention is a factor of ideological protection of the younger generation (socio-philosophical analysis). - T.: National Society of philosophers of Uzbekistan, 2019. P. 47.

formed and developed. This process is an objective necessity that arises from the meaning and essence of building a humane, just society.

Whichever nation and state borders on the development of a certain national aesthetic culture, which is formed in their territory, and leaves aside the role and role of other peoples, nations in Universal Civilization, then such signs as humanity, internationalism, the future of humanity, independence, mutual cooperation, friendship, brotherhood, which form the main basis of civil society, can be trampled on, as a result,

It should also be remembered that at a time when ideological conflicts are escalating and threats are growing on a global scale, it cannot be said that it is acceptable for everyone to follow this idea Permanently in our homeland. Some of our Ghanaians are very aware that national ideology is one of the most important factors in the prosperity of our motherland, and therefore, whatever they may be, they are trying to undermine the interethnic relations in our society and to empathize between them. "In today's era of globalization, the struggle for the acquisition of human consciousness and thinking is escalating, attempts to attract young people to the influence of foreign ideas and ideology, negative vices are gaining momentum, in a situation where our spiritual heritage and national values, which embody the dreams, aspirations and rich thinking of our ancestors, are becoming more relevant.[8]

Commenting on the strong veins of national ideology, Muhammad Quronov said, "they don't like the fact that we are growing together. For when we are one flesh and one soul, we shall not give our truth. If we do not come empty, they will not receive anything from us, even a large spike of our yantag , which is growing in our barren steppes.[9]" When we all rationally use examples of high aesthetic culture in our society, in which each person lives as like-minded and in harmony, our national ideology will continue to enrich its solid base.

In order to further strengthen such creative feelings in a person, the most noble qualities inherent in our national mentality, it is necessary that we are free from habits, skills and defects that

---

[8] Gaibullayev O. History and theory of national idea. - T.: "Science and technology", 2019. P. 163.
[9] Kuranov M. Glory be to your intention. "The word of the People", October 24, 2007.

have become "black legacies[10]" from the recent past and interfere with our pursuit of the future.

The main task facing the person is to protect the homeland, the joy of el-yurt, to live with his grief, to take the field as valor when work falls on el's head, to preserve the future of our country, the freedom of our people's erku, to protect its security, and also, "the main goal of the ideology is inextricably linked with the

Getting rid of these vices means building and elevating aesthetic awareness and national mentality. It is encouraging to develop visions such as national pride, a sense of pride, creativity, enthusiasm, love for the motherland and confidence in the prospect that resist these vices.

In our society, "the National idea has served as a factor that gives spiritual and spiritual strength in achieving noble dreams, goal-provisions. National ideology and ideology help to realize the important tasks facing all people, peoples, society and the state, and unite the people of the society operating in different areas and mobilize them towards a common goal" . In the National idea and ideology of our society, its

---

[10] Gaibullayev O. History and theory of national idea. - T.: "Science and technology", 2019. P. 297.

rarest and unique qualities, namely kindness, patience, andishness, disunity, sharmu-hayolik, elegance, sharp didiness, ibo-chastity, tolerance, hard work, humanism and other spiritual values, were embodied.

In each society, it will be possible to create some kind of national ideology on the basis of the interaction of certain national ideas with each other as a system. This is because while the National idea forms the basis of the national ideology, but it will consist of ideas as a specific system. From this idea it can be said that for the emergence of a national ideology, it is necessarily necessary that it be formed from certain national ideas and form into itself a system that affects the worldview of the individual.

First of all, it is not at all an amazing event that even one national idea applies as a national ideology in society. Such cases are common in human history. For example, in mysticism, the idea that each individual can unite with Allah in his own feeling has been important for several hundred years in his practical and spiritual life as a manifestation of the almost national ideology of our people. On the basis of this ideological creed, our people's faith in God and the feeling of honoring the beautiful landscapes of nature increased. He encouraged people to achieve truth through Sharia, enlightenment and sect, to purify them, and to some extent sought to unite them into the beauty of Allah. In social life, only a certain huge system of ideas can fulfill the task of having a strong influence on the psyche of an individual, reaching the heart of each of the people, moving them towards great and unified goals. It can be likened to the fact that bamisoli nature also shows people its beauty and that people enjoy it, impacting them not with one color, but with colors located in a certain order.

Secondly, Islam is recognized today as the most perfect religion on a global scale. It was in society that the emergence and formation of this religion was directly practiced as the national ideology of the Arab people. This ideology arose from the goals and interests, needs and aspirations of the Arab people alone, to unite and mobilize it in the works of goodness and creativity, Great Goals, not only the system of thousand-thousand ideas set forth in the Qur'an Karim and Hadith Sharif, but at the same time based on a number of practices such as fasting in the month of Ramadan, Currently, this ideology dominates the entire Muslim world. Therefore, the national ideology should, first of all, come as an ideological system and include in its composition not only a system made up of many national and non-national ideas, but also a system of certain actions.

Thirdly, in order for a national ideology to form as a holistic system, it is required not only to be formed from a certain number of ideas, but to place them in a certain order logically in line with each other, thereby complementing each other on the basis of their own content. In this, the national ideology will have such a new potential that now its influence on people will increase several times. Because every national idea in its composition is allowed to be perceived more persistently and vividly. As evidence of this, we will bring the main and Assamese ideas of the National idea of independence of our people. In this system of ideas, the main idea begins with the idea of a "free homeland", while the main idea begins with the idea of "peace of the land". The fact that this system of ideas begins with ideas of the same content is sequenced in a certain way, and finally from their unity as a system to a new meaning and meaning, as well as a huge idea of ideological significance, that is, a national ideology, arises.

Moreover, worldly knowledge, religious-divine values, enlightenment, philosophical observations about the perfect person, wisdom, freedom, justice, purity, honesty, Valor, patriotism, humanity, elegance, wise thoughts about the essence of Man, the meaning and meaning of human life, national and universal moral-aesthetic views, fairy tales and legends reflected in the healthy lifestyle, thinking and worldview of our people, the life of our national heroes, heroic deeds, etc., holds a place as base bases and sources. Indeed, this ideology determines the meaning and meaning of the long-standing noble aspirations, creative activities of our people. It embodies highly humane valued sides that are sacred to each person.

The priority and leading position of the national ideology in the development of the aesthetic culture of the individual in our society is evidenced by the fact that the independence of the Motherland is the basis of all our aspirations and lightness.

The national ideology of our people comes from the grounds that it should be formed from a number of ideas and put in such a sequence:

a) our people have lived under the conquests and oppression of various invaders-invaders for at least 2500 years for the next three thousand years. That is why the idea of a "free homeland" had become the sacred idea of our people with the highest meaning. The other three ideas have also taken shape in the minds and hearts of our people as their highest values for thousands to thousands of years, we are not mistaken. A.Ochildiev also believes that national ideology is a delicate issue with its long history. It is also controversial in society to "assess the process of formation of a national ideology as a long-term process, and to link its history to several millennia of balan. In this regard, we can see that with the improvement of the rules, principles, program guidelines set out in the national ideology in relation to the concrete historical conditions and situation, two mutually differentiating processes are mirrored, such as the formation of the national ideology as a system of ideological-theoretical views[11]" ;

b) Our people went through a great and extremely complex history, and therefore created

---

[11] Ochildieva. Milliyandamillatesaromunosabat. - T.: Uzbekistan, 2004. P. 12.

their national ideology in return. As a result, we were formed as a people with wisdom and high spirituality. Only a people of such wisdom and high spirituality can set himself the task of building a free and prosperous life, as the highest noble goal;

C) our people are formed on the basis of their national ideology as a public, a people inclined to live together. Each region is dominated by such qualities as the co-existence of citizens, consultation and business, elkadosh to each other in any wedding ceremonies in the neighborhood, loyalty to their national values, kindness, faith in Islam, care. There is another rare trait of our people that is, if it is also his humanity.

"It is not correct to understand the national ideology as the ideology of only one nation or people. It means the general ideology of a particular state or society. From this point of view, the concept of national ideology belongs to representatives of all nationalities living in Uzbekistan and operating in it[12]".

From this idea, it is known that ideology

---

[12] Yukilikov J.Ya., Mukhammadiev N.E. National idea: strategy for the development of Uzbekistan. - T.: Chulpan, 2018. P. 97.

under any circumstances serves as the basis for an idea with its Hox aesthetic, Hox moral, Hox political, Hox religious essence. On the basis of ideology, the idea enriches itself, connecting a new vision and teachings to the aesthetic culture of the individual.

Since national ideology serves to develop the aesthetic culture of the individual in our society, it cannot act as the ideology of the state at any time. It should be based only on the worldview of the people. We must all understand that these sentences are not the ideology of the national ideology we create as the state ideology, but the ideology of our people, which is aimed at the formation of the aesthetic culture of each individual in our society. On the basis of national ideology, the unification of the past and present of our people, their confidence and feelings for the future should develop as a force that gives aesthetic pleasure to each individual.

The formation of the aesthetic culture of the individual in the national spirit is fundamentally different from other ideologies by the fact that the national ideology we create can respond in every possible way. Because the essence of this ideology, the aesthetic culture and worldview of the individual in it, is formed in such a way that it is not based on any state intervention, directly following the principles of the power of the people, spiritual perfection, humanism. Today, " noble ideas in society at all times teach a person to live with high dreams, to fight faith in the path of noble goals. Humanity's ideas of justice, equality, peace, kinship, prosperity guided people towards higher goals on the basis of various religious and secular teachings. Islam, the Quran, and Hadith promoted the ideas of goodness about preserving nature, obtaining science, humanity, patriotism, honesty, spiritual purity, compassion, kindness, and righteousness, and glorifying parents and women[13]". It follows from this that in the national ideology, the fate of the historically composed people, the prospect of the land, the prosperous future of tomorrow of the nations harmonized with each other, the prosperity of a free and prosperous homeland are manifested.

While a number of scholars have expressed their views on the term national ideology, of which A.Erkaev says: "national ideology as a holistic system can be understood in two ways –

---

[13] Gaibullayev O. History and theory of national idea. - T.: Science and technology, 2019. P. 178.

narrowly and broadly... On the scale of society, one can judge each of the colorful ideologies as being private, and the national ideology as being common among them. This is a narrow understanding of national ideology. In broad terms, however, national ideology is the sum of the unique interpretation of an idea by different parties, groups, social strata, classes, pluralistic (colorful) views in society, theories[14]".

In this definition, it presents a diverse understanding of national ideology by humans. But the national ideology must embody the social environment of the individual, that is, the national and Universal, past and present, religious and secular aspirations that embody his being. Such aspects of national ideology are important in society. "One of the important tasks of the National idea and national ideology is to cultivate a sense of faith in the future, hope for a free and prosperous life. The National idea is based on national and universal principles. The fundamental interests of the nation, its assessment of its own past and its belief in the future are

---

[14] Erkaev A. The essence of the National idea. - T.: Spirituality, 2001. P. 15.

reflected in the National idea [15] ". In these opinions, the moral and aesthetic aspects of national ideology are defined in harmony with the social environment in society. We can also know a number of points in this regard.

Speaking about the content and essence of the national ideology in the formation of the aesthetic culture of the individual, the famous professor S.Mamashokirov says," when ideology becomes popular in society, ideas become real and self-regulated, a dynamic system – a living system-arises , consisting of a potentially developing social environment and conditions that move it.[16]" On the basis of this vision, the aesthetic culture of the individual develops on the basis of the dialectic of nationalism and generalism, bringing the dynamics of the driving forces of society into the field through cultural and spiritual culture. In it, the needs, goals and provisions of the people, their material and spiritual heritage, theoretical and practical activities are inextricably developed with an

---

[15] Gaibullayev O. History and theory of national idea. - T.: Science and technology, 2019. P. 291.
O masterpiece. P. 21.
[16] Mamashokirov S., Togaev Sh. Ideological and ideological issues of the construction of a free and prosperous life. - T.: Spirituality, 2007. P. 20.

aesthetic worldview embedded in the spirit of beauty.

While the philosopher emphasizes his definition of national ideology, he says that "national ideology will be a criterion that evaluates the processes of change in them: stages and levels of development; an organizing and coordinating mechanism; an action, a specific goal-guiding force – method-tool[17]", regulating the behavior of individual, social group v categories, the activities of all spheres and directions. These thoughts are philosophically researched that ideology is a necessary and universal process for the social environment of society.

The fact that national ideology is important for the development of society, its identity harmonizes with the spirit of the renewed era in the development of aesthetic culture.Musaev acknowledges:" the national ideology arises from the concept, from the theory that, looking at the state as the main subject of the process of democratic change, it is his active initiative that ensures the construction of civil society. "

---

[17] Musaev F. Philosophical and legal foundations of building a Democratic state. - T.: Uzbekistan, 2007. P. 222.

In these thoughts, the unity of national ideology with the social system is analyzed in connection with the modernity of a diverse worldview and ideas.

From these definitions and opinions given to national ideology, its connection with the whole history, reflecting the desires of the people, constantly developing, analyzing the ideas that dictate one another as a unifying force, can be defined as follows:

National ideology is the forms of social consciousness (moral political, religious, aesthetic spiritual, legal) based on the principle of humanism, which ensure the perfection of each individual in society, moving towards the future by connecting the past and present.) is the sum of, one might say.

The relationship of the national ideology with the aesthetic culture of the individual develops itself on the basis of a number of factors in the state arising from the philosophical and aesthetic aspects of civil society being built in Uzbekistan. These are:

- the manifestation of the aesthetic culture of the individual as the driving force of ideological processes of the object and the unity of the subject;

- ensuring the continuity of the aesthetic culture of the individual in the development of society with universal values on the basis of national ideology, promoting the increase in the role of spiritual heritage in the social environment;

- to carry out activities based on the content and essence of modernity in the absorption of the ideas of independence into the aesthetic consciousness of the individual;

- development of a system of measures aimed at increasing the role of a healthy lifestyle in society in the aesthetic culture of the individual on the basis of ideology;

On the basis of the harmonization of these factors with the aesthetic culture of the individual in society, a special ratio is given to ideological processes. On the basis of conformity with the spirit of the era, the aesthetic attitude of the individual to the national ideology forms colorfulness.

The influence of these factors on the psyche of the individual, the role in the development of aesthetic culture in society is associated with the fulfillment of tasks in society, their consideration at all levels in the process of education and upbringing, on the scale of society as a whole, the interaction of national and universal values, spirituality and national ideology.

Our national ideology, which embodied a new worldview and the spirit of the times in our society, has freed itself from views that are not inherent in the aesthetic culture of an existing person in the past, or rather in the former totalitarian regime. Because the spiritual image of this period had set itself the goals of building on a single ideology and managing society in a bureaucratic way. Analyzing such views," the only communist ideology that was the ideological basis of society during the period of the totalitarian regime was due to the fact that the peoples of our country, in particular the Uzbek people, did not take into account their lifestyle, worldview, history, customs, traditions and national characteristics, and the existence of a spiritual need to be different from its complications[18].

How relevant and extremely important the national ideology for our people, in which the

---

[18] National sovereignty of ideas and initiatives of the leader. –T.: Akademiya, 2007. 6-bet.

masterpieces of aesthetic culture form the basis of our spirituality, was thrown into the middle that each individual should be free from an old-fashioned worldview in civil society. In conclusion, national ideology is an important basis for the development and formation of the aesthetic culture of the individual in our society. In the rational and purposeful use of it, it is important to base aesthetic attitudes towards reality on a properly oriented Ridge, to ensure that each citizen operates on the basis of specific programs.

1.2§. The influence of aesthetic culture on a healthy lifestyle of ethnomethical and spiritual-ideological state in the Uzbek mentality

In the process of Social Development, a sacred ground is formed for any people or a person, inherited from their ancestors, which serves to mature and bring to adulthood the future generation, that is, the motherland and the national-spiritual values that will shoot a niche in its bosom and serve a prosperous life. This, in turn, leads to the fact that in society the ethnomanguage of an individual is manifested in social life in the manner of various traditions, udums and rituals between periods.

From the history of mankind, it is known that people who lived in different regions and territories at different times glorified their ancestral heritage and sought to develop them as high spiritual and ideological values. For each individual, the place where he was born and grew up is considered sacred, and his customs, local beliefs, have always been revered. In particular, "for Aborigines and other peoples living in the scorching desert – nomadic Bedouin, in lands covered with eternal glaciers – Evenks, living in impenetrable webs – the natural environment in which their ancestors passed and where they live, is the homeland of social space. He imagines his prosperity in the person of his family, bloodthirsty seeds, people's way of life, Faith, Dreams, living in his lawn, chalice, basement. The totality in these visions is a manifestation of the totality in spirituality[19]".

For the individual, it is in this natural environment that the formation of confidence, spirituality and ethnicity in the next day lies. In our country, this environment is called a family, in which spiritual and ideological situations that serve the upbringing of a human child as a person come first. In the Uzbek family there are traditions, values, traditions and rituals that are examples of a specific and appropriate ethnomathery, different from other peoples, each of which is one world. Simply putting a beautiful name on it when a child is born in a family is considered a tradition unique to our people. In this regard, it has been suggested that it is the duty of the parents to give the child a beautiful

---

[19] S. Mamashokirov, A. Utamurodov. The goal has been achieved. – T.: Editor, 2008. 17-bet.

name in Islam, as well as the "Kabusnoma"of Caicovus.

In the Uzbek people, in addition to universal concepts of elegance inherent in other peoples, there are spiritual and ideological situations that are inherent only in this people, forming an aesthetic culture of personality and society. There is a wide variety of opinions on this identity in many countries of the world: Russian political scientists say that "the family remains one of the most important life values, corresponding to the centuries-old traditions and mentality of Uzbeks.[20]" In fact, the Uzbek family, according to its tradition and history, has been raising its young people in the spirit of their upbringing, enjoying national elegance and ingenuity. Especially important in the upbringing of young people are the moral and aesthetic culture of older family members, such as taste, School of spiritual, feminine treatment, love of literature and art, neatness and striving for sincerity.

For example, in addition to being a vivid example of the national mentality of our people,

---

[20] Gafarli M.S, Kasaev A.Ch. Uzbek model of development: peace and stability – the basis of progress.- T.: Uzbekistan, 2001. P. 41.

femininity, national charm in the culture of letters, sayings and treats of the main characters in the novel "past days" by Abdullah Kadiri, serves as a huge example of the formation and development of the aesthetic culture of young people. In the words of this novel, "No one from this household has become unorthodox", our universal meanings and values are embodied.

Another Uzbek adibi Abdullah mentions the relevance of the role of upbringing in Avloni's thoughts about man. In his work "Turkish Gulistan or morals", he connects national-spiritual values for the development of a human child as a high person with aesthetic education, which is instilled in their minds. This is what he says about it:

Take a young bolosin of a bird,
The boilerplate is one way.
Anosin take asragan birla rum
Does not do, the man does the effort.
Should upbringing from a young age mean,
When it is great, it is necessary to grieve.
Egur the wretched man navdani,
The dam is egur burnt kavdani[21] .

---

[21] Avloni A. Turkish Gulistan or morality. - T.: Youth publishing house, 2018. P. 11.

Through these verses, Avloni says that the aesthetic culture of the individual begins with youth, it is difficult to educate a person after adulthood, to instill in his mind national-spiritual values. Also, Customs and rituals were considered important in the spiritual maturation of the individual, and it was important to raise national values in society, to develop enlightenment for the benefit of the people.

Avloni focused on the upbringing of the aesthetic culture of the individual, trying to ensure that he matured in society based on the observance of traditions, rituals and udums. This is explained by Avlony as follows:

God's mercy, Faizi hama yaksardur to man,
And but the condition for the upbringing to do with one is Akbar.
A child who cannot give birth, a painful punishment for you,
If your body is too strong, it will be a mercy for you.
If timurchi's child is raised, he will become a scientist,
If he is the son of Luqman, the future tyrant.
Joined the wicked son of Noah, became beimon,

Walked the old dog with hats, was horse man [22].

This indicates the presence of material and spiritual foundations in the rise of Avlonian national values at the base of the verses. It also tries to express the goals, aspirations of citizens living in society, to enrich the aesthetic culture of society. "History shows that every nation, every individual, must, first of all, have their own national pride, realize their identity. A person, a nation, first of all, respects other person, nations only when he respects himself. A proud nation that does not realize its existence will continue to live as a slave, no matter how much material wealth it has. On the contrary, the future of a nation that is conscious of its own, which venerates the history, value, customs, traditions of its ancestors will be great[23]". Therefore, it is difficult for us to honor all our traditions, traditions and rituals for the rise of the spiritual and ideological values of our people, which have lived unadorned for centuries, to bring up our youth with high human values.

The rich and unique spiritual and

---

[22] O masterpiece. P. 8.
[23] Azizhouzhaev A.A. Independence: struggles, anguish, joys. - T.: Academia. 2001. P. 8

ideological values of the Uzbek people abound, and in the formation of the aesthetic culture of the individual, they always form the meaning of their life. This particular manifestation of our spiritual heritage manifests itself in the person's delightful attitude to the aesthetics of marriage.

The aesthetic of a person's life develops on the basis of the family environment. In any family environment, a child from an early age sees his parents in his marriage and spends his life many times from the illusion that it will be in the same aesthetic culture way. He carefully observes all the events that take place in this environment, increasing his interest in life. Because, in this environment, a human child gradually matures his aesthetic attitudes towards reality. Remembering his interesting ideas every day, being in the company of many friends, a thousand come to the plane flying through the Immaculate Sky, immediately becoming a great man. It is natural that such household fantasies arise in the child's every question he gives to his parents. Seeing that his child aspires to a world of diverse ideas, the parent explains to him that all events and events in life take place one after the other, that one day the boy will also serve his people as a great man, becoming a highly civilized person in the future. Ana says that then the living conditions will fall on her shoulders and lead a beautiful family. While the parent admonishes his child, marriage enriches the ideals of taste, mind, sophistication in them, saying that life is rapidly changing and complex.

Aesthetic culture in the aesthetics of marriage develops in the family environment on the basis of imitation of the mother in many, and the father in boys. The aesthetics of married life in the family are taught to children, "children learn to work, the value of the thing he created, ... By making dolls for girls, making varrak for children, such skills emerge[24]", he argues.

However, a person tries to make his marriage beautiful with his aesthetic ideals, imagination, intelligence. Simply analyzing the fact that kitchen utensils also give decoration to a married person, various trays, trays, pots, bowls, kettles, bowls, spoons, etc.are avidly stored in apartments. These serve not only to satisfy the aesthetic need of a person, but also to make his marriage look beautiful, aesthetic culture.

---

[24] Abdullaeva N. Design and artistic-aesthetic culture. - T.: Turan-Iqbal, 2016. P. 87.

In the enrichment of the aesthetics of living, the aesthetic culture of the individual is greatly influenced by folk applied decorative art. After all, each person wants what satisfies his aesthetic need to be beautiful and aesthetically pleasing. For example, when choosing any furniture, table-chair, windows and doors, its convenience and beauty are taken into account. When the Mobado wants to equip the room, importance is attached to the beautiful decoration of its walls, the beauty of the window curtains, the aesthetic appearance of the items to be placed in the room.

In a person's marriage, the aesthetic strength of folk applied decorative art is so great that it reflects the diverse peat worlds, beautiful patterns and ornaments of people about the universe, landscapes of nature with a colorful appearance. This is how attractive landscapes and views on reality, improving the culture of the individual, give rise to their aesthetic relationship about the universe with its long and eternal fronts. Therefore, the aesthetics of living should serve for the development of the main aesthetic culture of Uzbek households in the process of building civil society today.

In the aesthetics of marriage, the entire inner and outer qualities of the individual are manifested. The development, formation of a culture of personality circulation is perfected, first in the family, in the environment of family members, and later in kindergarten, neighborhood, school, Lyceum, College, higher educational institutions and public institutions. Since the initial focus of the culture of circulation is the family, we must all teach our children to always be aesthetically civilized, that is, to speak beautifully, to avoid bad and ugly words. Because the Hadith Sharifs, an example of a high aesthetic culture, also say in this regard: "a good word is a soul, a bad word is a pile of language", "one's beauty is known from his language", "a person commits error more with his own language", "tenderness is the beginning of wisdom", "avoid a sentence that sounds bad to the ear", etc.

Consequently, we must all raise our culture of treatment high in the system of pleasure relations, teach our youth the words that positively affect our psyche, promote that the purpose of living is to grow up to be a person of high aesthetic culture. As long as a person lives, he still feels an exposure to circulation, whether he wants it. This requires him to be aesthetically cultured, that is, sweet and sincere, to be imaginative and diabolical, chaste and charming of our daughters, and to be polite, courteous, valiant, courageous, alert and human.

A large role in the formation of the aesthetic culture of the individual is played by the issues of adherence to cleanliness in the family, order and order. It's mukin that everyone does it. But taste in a person is diverse in different areas of Labor aesthetics, based on the aesthetics of different lives. Therefore, there will never be a person without taste, but the aesthetic taste and ideals of people in maintaining cleanliness, observing cleanliness, keeping the household in order are colorful. Because everyone has good or bad, beautiful or ugly taste. Aesthetic taste is in the purity and height of consciousness and understanding of these people, and not only in how much the O'kighan books, the cinema they see, or in the clothes they wear. Therefore, the aesthetic culture of the individual determines its true beauty through aesthetic taste, serving to make the spiritual life rich, to keep the individual clean, tidy, pure, humble, constantly paying attention to himself, to be in order.

The family is also delightful for each individual to dress selectively in simple and elegant attire, to be tasteful and ingenious. This, on the one hand, makes the aesthetic culture of the individual unobtrusive and presentable, on the other hand, leads to low output for the family, not increasing spending, not cools excess money into the street, making the family strong.

The bulk of the living conditions arise in relation to the marriage of young people, that is, their wedding. The wedding is one of the long-standing ceremonies that love the soul of the Uzbek people. In all neighborhoods where the wedding will take place, a relative-a seed and a cow-is gathered before the wedding and a "consultation oshi" is organized. In it, those who come to the wedding as an aid to the wedding owner begin the wedding in harmony, seeking their blessing and taking on part of the expenses of the wedding. When the wedding begins, the hosts, marked by a neighborhood elder, are belted from a waistband to warmly welcome guests to the wedding. Especially in the apartment where the wedding is taking place, joy on Joy, wish the young people a lifetime of happiness will be noble wishes in the first Gal.

Having just understood what an independent life is before the start of the wedding, the guy and the girl are delighted with the moments of marriage, which will be once in a lifetime, and sign the necessary legal documents to become a couple associated with going through the registry office (writing civil status documents). These are all the most exciting, memorable moments of happiness of the young bride and groom for a lifetime, as well as beautiful and harmonious moments of life, which are called a family.

These will be followed by the wonderful wedding of the happy bride and groom. At the wedding, all people have fun, cheer, wish happiness to the young bride and groom. This is how the aesthetics of Uzbek weddings were born. The greater the number of weddings in Uzbek apartments is a sign of the goodness of our marriage, the way our children step into an independent life, their whole life should be filled with flowers like a beautiful spring season and live a happy life, our young people should live with each other always understood. All this gives rise to our aesthetic culture based on the aesthetics of marriage.

In later times, there have been cases of Su'is'temolization of aesthetic culture when conducting wedding luxuries and maracas. We see this thing more especially at Bridal weddings. At the wedding of Tashkent and Samarkand, the hosts el-yurt, who have released more of them because of the upcoming weddings, call for a girl in exchange for a loan, saying that she will not die in front of the neighborhood (the chariots) are making their wedding. As a result, the borrowed wedding has to suffer for several years. As a result, there are also cases of violation of the moral and aesthetic criterion in the conduct of certain customs, rituals. Violation of the moral and aesthetic criterion can also lead to various negative consequences.

In order to eliminate such cases, the Joint Resolution No. 2736-III/KQ-592-III of the Council of the Legislative Chamber of the Republic of Uzbekistan and the Senate of the Republic of Uzbekistan dated September 14, 2019 "on further improvement of the system of regulation of weddings, family celebrations, ceremonies and ceremonies"noted: "in recent years, reflecting the long-standing values and traditions of our people, vices such as disregard for the social situation of others, extravagance, disregard for the Customs and traditions of our people are conspicuous " . Such lavish rituals and marakas negatively affect the consciousness of the individual, undermine the healthy growth of his moral and aesthetic culture and taste.

In recent years, in some married New families, the commandment is also being mastered to understand the emergence of warfights with various excuses over a trifle.

The youth of a person flows like water. Girls get married, guys get married. As a result, Family anxiety, child rearing and other marriage-related responsibilities begin. They go through the bittersweet, good-bad days of marriage. It is at this moment that the couple must be one and share together what they have found, enriching the Holy See of the family with aesthetic praise. At this time, the couple tries each other, overcoming mutual difficulties. When the wife, who always received clothes, was told to her husband's comments, " did you make money and dress up?", "My parents are taking it","Am I getting clothes for your money, making it myself and finding it myself"? saying something like that will increase the pain of a young man who is crushed internally by the circumstances that have arisen in the family. But especially if you say this in love and get married! In such cases, negative consequences can arise in the family. Therefore, every guy-girl should patiently cope with the heaviness and lightness of marriage, good-bad days, make their lives rich in wonderful miracles that people envy.

Some families have young adults who have grown up to be erkatoy. These should be taught by parents to express their pandemics, to solve all the sweet and ugly situations that will happen in the Holy circle as a family as a couple. On this basis, the noble feelings of the individual, the aesthetic ideals, imagination, concepts of the Uzbek people, who sing their human qualities, are formed in a common way with an invaluable and unique past dependence on inheritance. On this basis, the aesthetic ideals of a person who is thoughtful and kind, sociable and hardworking, will always be rich and more mature. For this reason, the Uzbek people rely on their ancient and rich aesthetic ideals without hesitation in the upbringing of young people with a bright and energetic, comprehensively spiritual maturity. The aesthetic ideals of the individual create a commonality with the concept of aesthetic culture, bringing them closer to each other. And the fact that such aesthetic ideals differ in different people is naturally an expression of the complex and multifaceted nature of man.

The aesthetic culture and aesthetic ideals of the individual living in each society cannot be the same. It is this person's attitude to life, his goals and aspirations that indirectly indicate his dependence on the aesthetic ideal.

Today, it is the desire of every young person to get married and mature a prosperous family on the basis of high and pure aesthetic ideals, which are overwhelmed by Sacred feelings. Therefore, before fulfilling their desires, young people should be guided by their manners, behavior, attitude towards the motherland, to the land, to the parents, to the brother. Only a nation that has realized its identity in the path of community prosperity will always be able to have a novelty, a modern worldview, the development of social life. In this situation, each individual seeks to develop his own delightful attitude to values, customs, traditions and rituals in connection with the spiritual world.

In the process, we can see that our people's

faith in Islam and high aesthetic culture are strong. But in later times we can also see that there are attempts to make them Su'is'temol instead of raising our religious values in this matter. In some places, people are associated with each other without a proper understanding of the differences between national customs and religious rituals. Local customs contrary to Sharia in places are sought to be included in the ritual order. After the death of Man, "the funeral ceremony began to be given to the dead by reciting the Quran, blessing them at events such as 7, 20, 40, yil, hayit, snow fell. From then on, they were taken as a religious ritual and performed as if they were obligatory or circumcised practices. Later, holding such ceremonies with large feasts, as at weddings, became an urf. But the"regulations on the regulation of weddings, family celebrations, Ma'raka and ceremonies "states that" funerals and mourning ceremonies can be held in the presence of an unlimited number of Citizens for a maximum of three days, except for the ceremony of giving soup". Therefore, neighborhood concubines should have a deep understanding of preventing excessive pomp and ambition in funerals.

We need to explain to the general public that they do not waste too much pomp and grudges, do not torment themselves with unnecessary spending. We must all be united in ensuring the solidarity of our people in the conduct of the Ramadan Eid and Qurban Eid, the main holidays of the Islamic religion. It is a sign of high humanity and aesthetic culture in our religion to receive messages from the elderly on our religious holiday, to go and see the sick, to help widows and families in need of help.

Before these holidays, it is important to clean the cemeteries where our ancestors headed for eternal life. In this regard, our Prophet Muhammad expressed his thoughts and said that death and life, cleaning cemeteries, visiting passersby are a force that positively affects the aesthetic culture of the individual and will be an example of a lesson. They bless this in their Hadith: "I forbid you from visiting the graves, and now visit, and visiting the graves will bring death to mind[25]".

The veneration of tombs among our people,

---

[25] The idea of national independence and the activities of the leader. - T.: Academia, 2007. P. 65.

the constant desire to clean and purify them, has become one of our long-standing traditions. Our ancestors revered cemeteries from time immemorial as a place of great importance, a place of pilgrimage, where the dead lay. It was considered sinful to throw waste at the grave, to hold ablutions, to sit on the cave dung, even to pray here. Inside the cemetery, it was forbidden to run, press them, play the boy Baccarat. When the horse-mounted men came close to the grave, they descended from the saddle and walked softly, leading their mounts until they moved away from the territory of the cemetery, so as not to disturb the spirit of the deceased. It is also a symbol of our honor that we take the blessing in front of the cemetery, saying "May the dead be thanked by God". In the case of our people, it is also sinful to count the graves, to make them big with a finger.

  Therefore, all of us must always honor the religious rites and traditions of our ancestors that we have inherited from generations, and preserve them as awe-inspiring as eyebrows. Religious values should be used wisely in the formation of the aesthetic culture of the individual. Especially important in the family are the attitude of the couple towards each other, humanity in their treatment, kindness, an equally responsible approach to the upbringing of children, their unfaithfulness towards each other.

The role of spiritual and ideological values in the formation of aesthetic culture of the individual in society is important. The emergence of these values is formed in traditions and rituals of material, spiritual, cultural riches, certain territorial integrity, national language, moral relations in society, customs, created in the process of long historical development. "In this respect, our customs, rituals and traditions have a positive significance as a kind of component of our nationality, which determines our national-spiritual image, interprets our national characteristics and qualities to the world.[26]"

The fact that our spiritual and ideological values acquire a unique national character leads to the formation of patterns of aesthetic culture of an individual. This, in turn, " in our country, the interest of the population in National-traditional types of creativity (folk art, art-ethnographic associations, tea houses, cultural recreation, physical recreation, public holidays) is growing.

---

[26] Musaev F. Building a Democratic state-financial-legal basis. - T.: Uzbekistan, 2007. Pp. 69-70.

In particular, the restoration, preservation and development of national cultural heritage and the enrichment of Culture, interesting leisure, winding up the traditions of our ancestors, instilling affection for them in the younger generation are turning voluntary associations into widespread national democratic institutions. Many established Guzars, cultural-spiritual centers, workshops built on the traditions of the teacher-disciple, associations more broadly manifest national-ethnic characteristics in civil society[27]".

In the pleasure relationship to national values in a period that is shaping civil society, it is permissible to say that sometimes negative aspects of different types of practical activities, goh transparent, goh pinhona, are entering our social life. Today we can also meet such people in all regions of our republic (more residential and cultural recreation areas, tea houses). They are striving to spend their free time not in order to improve the upbringing of a family or children, lifestyle, but simply by watching films of gambling, stupidity, drunkenness, moral

---
[27] Karimov I.A. High spirituality is an invincible force. - T.: Spirituality, 2008. P. 58.

perversion. Having talked with such people, he is ashamed to openly show such features in his act, hide it, strive to lose it. This feature is universal and is a great force in the hands of society in the fight against bad traits, in the upbringing of the younger generation as the owner of real human qualities. The natural aspiration for good, beauty, moral perfection in people comes into play in the fight against bad characteristics in the morality of people, in their loss, in the future, in the upbringing of them competently, encourages a perfect confident view of the victory of the Society of man.

In the formation of the aesthetic culture of personality and society, "Customs and traditions inherent in our people, such as mutual Kindness, Harmony and harmony, lack of need, receiving messages from the people in need of help, stroking the heads of orphans, holding weddings, hashar and Ma'rakas with many, being together both on a good day and on a bad day," have maintained its eternity for thousands of years.

The role of family rituals is growing with the creation of a wide range of opportunities for the development of traditions and traditions of our people, coexisting on the basis of community in the neighborhoods. The acquisition of independence paved the way for the restoration of the traditions of many of the family rituals that were forbidden during the time of the shawls, such as the chunonchi, "naming", "charlar", "hair wedding", "tooth wedding", "cradle wedding", "circumcision wedding", "muchal wedding". This case is definitely positive. But in the following years, the restoration of a simple family ceremony and traditions is formed by the feeling of ownership of "who is the other". Negative vices such as ambition, pomp, self-indulgence, indulgence, and indulgence are prominent in these rituals.

In order to create a person with a high aesthetic culture among our people, we all need to be united, united and strive to increase the spiritual maturity of the younger generation, be aware of ideas that are far from our mentality and remove them from our rituals. Some families, in particular, spend a lavish and extravagant wedding with exorbitant expenses, while low-cost families suffer from children's rations and end up in debt. Some ceremonies, such as the" cradle wedding", the" circumcision wedding", are being transformed into grand celebrations instead of being held between family, neighbours and relatives.

The customs of the wedding ceremony, such as "bread break", "advice oshi", "call in the blood", "girl bazmi", "opened a face", "the bride saw", "Bride choirs", "bridal call", are becoming separate events. It is advisable to spend them in a compact form, with the participation of family members, close relatives, without excessive pomp and large expenses. Ceremonies such as "birthday parties", "cradle weddings", "circumcision weddings", which are turning into a big wedding in places, are also welcome to be celebrated as a small, compact family event in the company of relatives and neighbors. Excess rituals such as" the dress saw"," sarpo wrote"," the smoke returned"," the door opened " should be abandoned.

Traditions and rituals in such a community-based environment are grandiose for each individual, inherited from generation to generation, from parent to child, in which national-cultural values manifest their height more persistently and clearly. In this neighborhood environment, the consciousness and thinking of the individual is formed and matured. The example of a person's high aesthetic culture seeks to seal into the future the national-cultural values enriched by the spirit of the times in national customs and traditions, rituals and traditions.

Today we must live in harmony with the times in order to rationally use national-spiritual values, traditions, traditions and rituals, which are an important factor in the rise of aesthetic thinking and culture of the individual. The main reason for this is the strong and rapid absorption of destructive ideas into the human mind in" the influence of information space, which in some cases contradicts our traditions and traditions, national ideological foundations, due to events and phenomena related to the life of different peoples, nations, music, dance and songs.[28]"

In such conditions, we must serve the National-Spiritual rise of society as a branch of the infinite peat universe, which recognizes national and universal values for every young man-girl, forms as a person and shows itself.

As a result of the emergence of a wide range of activities in our society for the rise of the

---

[28] National sovereignty of ideas and initiatives of the leader. –T.: Akademiya, 2007. 79-bet.

aesthetic culture of the individual, our national and cultural values strive to embody universal.

The rise of the aesthetic culture of society and the individual is enriched by the fact that it is based directly on life experiences formed on the basis of spiritual and ideological values, striving to express noble intentions and goals in itself. The aesthetic needs of the individual, as an endless process, manifest their flashy manifestations, serving to practice traditions and rituals in society in an updated way. This process required us to mature our national heritage, spiritual and ideological values, which will lead to the formation of an aesthetic culture, which will be based on high spirituality and enlightenment, arising from the interests and demands of the state and society. Because the strong faith of our people is polished on the basis of these values and seeks to develop its SERM'no image. This national heritage has long been the sum of such spiritual assets as our ancestors, ancestors, political, philosophical, legal, national and religious values, moral standards, achievements of science, historical, artistic and artistic works, which our people have always studied and enriched. Therefore, all ethnomathean traditions, deeds and rituals have also demanded a culture of treatment in our land, which is based on unity, harmony, co-existence, interethnic harmony, cowardice, sincerity.

From time immemorial, the culture of treatment has developed in our country in a way that harmonizes with aesthetic culture, listening to each other between individuals or nations, respecting thoughts aimed at any goodness in activities in the interests of society and the state, taking into account the prospect of the land, trying to solve the problem in each situation with heaviness and restraint.

The aesthetic worldview, spiritual world, and perceptions of social life of people of different nationalities living in the same land can be diverse, but there is a great deal of affinity in their aesthetic cultures, namely science, education, culture, and art. The individual may not "follow certain customs and traditions of the nations living in the same territory, based on their spiritual and ideological values, but should look at them with respect and not laugh at them, not Myna" . Because there is a national value of each nation, which means its own, which indicates its difference from other nations, and another member of society reacts to it based on his own worldview.

Ethnomathean traditions and rituals, traditions, which are the spiritual and ideologues of their ancestors in the development of each people, always want to be appreciated. The law of social progress is such that the language, customs of each nation are very valuable to themselves! A person speaks his language freely, thinks freely in his own language. On the other hand, the customs inherited from their ancestors are their sacred wealth, their pride, their or-name, or, if permissible, their immortal memories. Therefore, denigrating the language or customs of another nation is equivalent to insulting this nation. Thus, such an image attracted every citizen of our people to his domain in the era of former salons. This cult, forgetting about itself, sought to seal the fate of all peoples who united not only Uzbekistan, but also a large empire. Their task was" to move the Rusi-zabon nation to Uzbekistan with various slander, to consistently increase their number and number, to instill in our people the Russian language, customs, traditions, values and lifestyle.[29]" Of these negative changes in the lifestyle of our entire people, only our countrymen living in the village were saved by the factor that made up the majority of the general population. In large cities, the Russian way of life, the Customs and traditions of the language ensured its priority" . But it should also be said that zamona, according to Zaili, was forced to live without renouncing the nationality of our people, who had a good understanding of their identity, the national values and aesthetic culture of their ancestors.

The Eastern spiritual and ideological, rich and harmonious, philosophical-aesthetic landscape of the Farb world also dates back to the new century. Many opinions have been expressed about the positive aspects of the peculiarities of the eastern worldview, which are taking shape in the psyche of the pharbees.

As a result of the important features of human aesthetic culture in the new century, today the Farb world realizes that adherence to the ideas of individualism will be rich in problems for the life of an individual. In this regard, the Farb

---

[29] Ziemukhammadov B. Complete the book. –T.:" Turon-iqbol " publishing house, 2006. 250-bet.

researcher is an English scientist A. comparing their views to those of the East, Etsioni writes that people "now understand that individualism does not conform to principles[30]". This, in turn, serves to enrich the national and modern Ana'anas, cultural lifestyle, moral ideals of the Orientalist, who does not always lose the value of time for the aesthetic culture of the individual.

There are examples of such an aesthetic culture embedded in the blood vessels of our people that do not directly affect the social lifestyle of each individual. We can also know the secret of such a kind of Customs and rituals through the "Navruz", a national holiday that expresses the equality of day and night. This holiday also serves as a bridge that serves to convey the past and aesthetic culture of our unique people to the future.

There are many methods and tools for the formation and development of a new aesthetic culture in the personality mind: "the idea of national independence: basic concepts and principles", as noted in the book "traditions, rituals and holidays that have been formed over

---

[30] Sadullah Otamurotov, Sarvar Otamurotov. Spiritual and spiritual revival of Uzbekistan. –T.: Young Ages, 2003.194-195-betlar.

the centuries, passed down from generation to generation[31]." an invaluable legacy will also be an important factor, in particular, it is necessary to use our holidays and rituals, such as Independence, Navruz, teachers and coaches, the day of memory and appreciation, wisely in the way of giving modern meaning to the life of society.[32]"

Based on these, the aesthetic culture of each person covers areas such as "spiritual-cultural life, educational education, cultural heritage, historical experience, religious, moral, educational views, lifestyle, colorful relationships, science, folk holidays, parties, performances and events, art, literature. The distinctive ethnic characteristics of the people, the nation, their contribution to world civilization are also actually measured by these spiritual and cultural values."The development of attractive and unique spaces of aesthetic culture is a product of democratic reforms carried out in our republic, in which national and cultural values, which are considered valuable to each person, serve to

---

[31] Etsioni A. The Spirit of Community. Rights and Responsibilities and the Communitarian Agenda. - London: 1995. –P. 24.
[32] The idea of national independence: basic concepts and principles. - T.: 2001. P. 177.

demonstrate to the world the wealth of the spiritual world of Uzbekistan with its universal and humane nature. As a result of this, " the national democratic changes carried out in Uzbekistan, on the second hand, support the customs of the people, their values formed in the process of socio-historical development, encourage them to preserve them as national-cultural assets, to make good use of them in their formation. new generation. In which country, no matter what social space is carried out, literal democracy cannot reject its Ana'anawi values under the banner of modernization, changes that do not rely on evolutionism do not occur in the way of life, in the soul of people.[33]"

In order for a person to mature in our society in every possible way, we must first of all pay special attention to the ANA'anas, national values, udum and rituals that form the basis of historically formed religious and secular knowledge. This implies that each individual relies on objective and subjective factors in society. These factors always require universal values if their people are raised to the level of

---

[33] Musaev F. Philosophical and legal foundations of building a Democratic state. - T.: Uzbekistan, 2007. P. 119.

deep perception of the spirituality of another nation and, on the contrary, have the opportunity to freely and unconsciously demonstrate their national dignity without intentions other than friendly economic and spiritual communication in national relations. the spirituality of different peoples will continue to grow.

The development of spiritual and ideological values in society directly creates factors that serve the rise of a person's specific national worldview and aesthetic culture:

- ethnomathean Ana'ana and values influence the aesthetic consciousness and thinking of an individual in society in a national and universal spirit, developing a pleasant attitude to the activities taking place in each area;

- on the basis of spiritual and ideological values, a number of nationalities and elates living in a certain area unite and form a spiritual and aesthetic worldview aimed at ensuring the aesthetic culture of society and the well-being of the people;

- when carrying out any activities guaranteed by law by the state, ethnomathean traditions and Customs serve to provide no courtesy of their nation;

- The process of developing an aesthetic culture of a person, which covers interethnic relations, united directly in the path of prosperity of the motherland, makes every citizen peaceful, capricious, patriotic, compatriot, hardworking, benevolent, noble, kind, devoted, faithful, morally pure conscientious, humble and humble;

- Ana'ana, udum, serves as the basis of spiritual and ideological values in society, and rituals serve to form a perfect person who leads everyone to goodness as an important part of folk spirituality;

- as a result of the rise of the aesthetic culture of the individual, an aesthetic heritage arises, which ensures the decision-making of modern democratic values in relation to historical heritage and philosophical thought.

When analyzing the connection of human aesthetic culture with nationalism in society, we will have to focus on aspects of its connection with the process of historical development, study what the ideology and aesthetic world of that time were in folk thought, take into account historical conditions. At the moment, we strive to create a period when we realize our self, to build changes in the field of aesthetic culture with high spirituality.

This period entails the creation of continuous programs and laws aimed at the bright prospect of Uzbekistan, the foundation of reforms in social life on the principle of "national revival – national ascension". Such a requirement is currently being implemented in stages in all areas of society.

The new image of the aesthetic culture of a person taking place in our society shows that reforms serve the interests of a person, democratic principles become richer and sweeter, the goal of our spiritual world is a person with high spirituality. As the driving force of this process, we must look for ways to achieve that the foundation of the relationship between "person and society", "person and State", "person and Idea", "person and ideology", "person and nation" is an aesthetic culture. feel deeply that dreams of building a beautiful life lie at the heart of each study. The tag-stem of this activity should be absorbed into the spiritual world of the individual, enriched with masterpieces of aesthetic culture and turn it into a masterpiece of beauty.

Today, in the formation and development of an individual aesthetic culture, there is no more reliable source than habits, images, traditions-a rich and unique moral-spiritual, spiritual-aesthetic golden heritage. Because all this with the inclusion of Sergio Faiz in the aesthetic vision of the individual, with its confident and aesthetic nature, has always increased its self-esteem for centuries.

As the heirs of a new society, we must always preserve the masterpieces of aesthetic thinking higher than this, deliver them in their own way to future generations, introduce rare manuscripts and works of aesthetic culture created by our ancestors to the whole world, demonstrate how rich and attractive our past has always been moving forward in the field of Science and culture.

1.3§. Constructive significance of art in the formation of aesthetic culture in the Uzbek mentality.

The role of art and sports is great in the fact that every person grows up to be a mature perfect person in radiating purity and innocence, goodness and light rays into the psyche of the people. The roots of any aesthetic culture that takes shape in society lie directly in harmony with the constructive aspects of art.

Art is a mirror of the spiritual life of a certain period, in which the life of a nation, national traditions, modern social progress reflect the individual characteristics, nature and worldviews of individuals in artistic images. The result of this process gives an artistic-aesthetic picture of the people's consciousness and, especially, the imagination and activity of the individual, serving to the realization of the qualities of creativity and creativity in them.

The full realization of such a social function of art should be the content of free creativity and labor laws in society. In the era of ideological soloism of the last century, such freedom, the principles of the inherent internal progress of art were not allowed. Art was transformed into a communist ideology and its program promoter. Individual capacities were limited by certain norms of the creative style, and as a result, the principles of socialist realism prevailed.

From the first days of independence, the task of re-perception of previous creative searches and successes in artistic and aesthetic activities, the creation of artistic values corresponding to the spirit, consciousness of our new national statehood and our country, people was put on the agenda. In the years of independence, changes also began to occur in the artistic-aesthetic consciousness, based on the principles of reforming in all spheres of social life, restoring national values, changing and updating human thinking. True, sharp changes in social life did not go directly into the world of artistic creativity. The freedom of the individual, which was kept in custody for a long time, had to adapt to a new social system and new spiritual needs, creating monand artistic images for him.

Before the artists who gained social and creative freedom, the responsibility arose to instill in the people's consciousness these aesthetic feelings, feeling the fundamental essence of the freedom of the people and The Motherland, which has been dreamed of for centuries. Instead of the previous abstract and national life, spiritual values far from ideal, the task of chanting an independent homeland, the history of an independent people, historical memory, rich heritage and traditions, aspirations in artistic images took place from the agenda. In such a socio-political and libertarian context, there have also been cases of inadequate awareness of their ideological principle. It was during this period that certain aspects of the ideological gap were found in the media.

Our first president Islam Karimov, speaking at the first session of the Supreme Council of the Republic of Uzbekistan of the twelfth convocation (March 24, 1990), warned that "there has been an increase in the promotion of obscenity in art on television, film screens, in the media of the press, of obscenity, absurdity and shamelessness, and sometimes even moral perversion.[34]"

It was a natural case that such examples of

---

[34] Karimov I.A. On the path of spiritual elevation. - T.: Uzbekistan, 1998. P. 28.

art did not correspond to our national mentality, spiritual heritage and moral values.

Consequently, before the people of art stood the task of creating patterns of artistic creativity that shape and develop the artistic and aesthetic thinking and culture of our people, creating a new modern history, related to the fate of the nation and the country.

From the date of the declaration of independence, a wide range of reforms in the political, economic and spiritual spheres have flared up in Uzbekistan. First of all, ensuring the peace, stability and well-being of the country became the main goal. Because" music does not enter the ear of a hungry person, that is, even if you agitate for him a thousand times, he does not think of anything other than his belly.[35]" At a time when temporary economic difficulties, the existence of various views and moods in the process of national recovery and purification, the direction of spiritual life and the principles of reforming the educational system became a social necessity, a huge responsibility was placed on the people of literature and art.

---

[35] Karimov I.A. Uzbekistan: national independence, economy, politics, ideology. - T.: Volume 1, Uzbekistan, 1996. P. 210.

Little is found in the power and factor that strongly influences the consciousness and imagination of the people, a piece from literature and art, bringing it to the peak of high spirituality. Because " when you read great poems, you get some kind of pride, a sense of pride, that a person feels capable of everything, both spiritually and physically.[36]" Thanks to this, the aesthetic culture of the individual becomes richer with new inspirational ideas.

Therefore, strengthening the aesthetic culture of the people in creating new literature and art of the independence era has become an important social issue in order to preserve independence, to bring it to life to future generations, to properly explain its value to our people, to restore our national artistic tradition and heritage, to raise our national consciousness and raise our

Since independence was gained in a time when society faced a national-spiritual crisis, our language, religion, cultural heritage and traditions were found, it was a great socio-philosophical task to convey to the people through artistic images how much it was a necessary social

---

[36] Karimov I.A. O masterpiece. P. 210.

phenomenon for the prospect of our country and our people, and to educate the younger generation in the spirit of Our people have long been fond of fiction, art, through which the generation that enjoys universal values has always been the most progressive, most perfect generation. Literature is one of the means of ensuring the elevation, perfection of human spirituality. His main idea is also to glorify a person, to promote goodness, justice, Free, truly human friendship, compassion. On its basis, unique examples of art and images and aesthetic culture aimed at ensuring the full maturity of the individual are reflected, which, in turn, take place from the artistic-aesthetic consciousness and thinking of the people's masses.

Enriching, nurturing a politically awakened people, especially every individual, now nationally and universally spiritually, from the breeze of independence, was put on the agenda as the most important task. Therefore, the reforms carried out in our country were carried out not first in the sense of economy, then spirituality, but in harmony and communication, not separating them from each other. Reforms in the field of spirituality and aesthetic culture began, first of all, to create the legal foundations of the activities of the people of creative labor, to give them free creativity, to create new and new opportunities for creative development. Accordingly, the creators were also assigned tasks arising from the requirements of the ideology of independence.

As long as there was an opportunity for the restoration of our oriental ethics, traditions, system of tradition and upbringing, spiritual and aesthetic values, there was a prerequisite for a change in creative intentions and activities. Now the educational system had changed towards the realization of the national self and the development of the national roots of artistic creativity. It was necessary that the little children also know and enjoy the images of Uzbek folk tales, our traditional puppet theater, without knowing or recognizing only the heroes of Walt Disney, Winnie The Pooh or "nu, pogodi". Because the emergence, presentation of tasteless, artistically shallow and ideologically smokeless works undermined the upbringing of young people in the spirit of Holy ideas associated with independence. Therefore, the TV channel "Boyjon" was created, which corresponds to the psyche, spiritual world of our children. This, in turn, has become a great aesthetic cultural treasure for our little ones, a school for the formation of literacy aimed at gaining knowledge.

In parallel with them, there was a need for literature and art that would educate young people with patriotism, truthfulness, truthfulness, politeness, in short, a bone-hardened generation with Oriental morals and universal values. This literature has become very important in the formation of Free Speech, Free Thought and a free human worldview, its artistic and aesthetic culture. The works created by free creators of a free society began to serve the spiritual revival of the people, the upbringing of their aesthetic culture. The anthem of Uzbekistan, created by Abdulla Oripov and Mutal Burkhanov, was a great socio-political and artistic-aesthetic event in the rise of our spirituality.

The glare of the coat of arms, flag and anthem of Uzbekistan at political, sports and cultural events, khilpirashi and echoes are constantly filling the heart and consciousness of our people with bright emotions, delightful feelings, serving as a huge spiritual factor in the aesthetic education of our youth.

If we imagine the measures taken during

the past period for the development of literature and art, the conditions created and the masterpieces of culture, we will witness that centuries of unfulfilled work has been carried out in this area. Independence gave a new spirit to the aesthetic culture of the individual, saying that "with the care of the leader of the country, in addition to the new construction of cultural and art structures, huge cultural and historical monuments left by our ancestors are also being renovated again. For this purpose, more than twenty decrees and resolutions are adopted, which find their implementation. These documents serve as a means of legal basis in the development of our nation's culture, art, as well as our national spirituality[37]".

In recent years, the Khumo Arena ice sports palace in Tashkent alone, the history of Uzbekistan channel as part of the National Broadcasting Company of Uzbekistan, branches of 14 universities and institutions of such a state as South Korea, Great Britain, Russia, India, Italy, Singapore, Latvia, the 700th anniversary of the great alloma Bahovuddin Naqshband grandfather,

---

[37] The idea of national independence and the activities of the leader. - T.: Academia, 2007. Pp. 46-47.

the 145th birthday celebrations of the enlightened and public figure Mahmudkhoja Behbudy, are contributing.

The decree of the president of the Republic of Uzbekistan Shavkat Mirziyov on literature, art and culture is a sign of how great importance spirituality and enlightenment are in the education of the human perfection, the harmonious generation:" on measures for the further development and improvement of the culture and art sphere"(may 31, 2017)" on measures for the further improvement of the activities of the Union of writers of Uzbekistan "; (April 5, 2018); "on measures to promote the innovation of culture and art in the Republic of Uzbekistan" (August 26, 2018);" on measures to prepare for the holding of the international music festival" taronas of the East "(February 26, 2019);" on measures to promote and fund the implementation of Public-Private Partnership in culture and arts " (July 9, 2019); "Children's music and art schools on remuneration for the work of leaders, teachers and concertmasters and improving the system of their material incentives"(September 30, 2019);" on measures for the further development of national dance art "(February 5, 2020);" on measures to further improve the effectiveness of the field of fine and Applied Arts " (April 21, 2020), etc.

All decrees aimed at raising the spirituality of our people and the aesthetic culture of the individual, as well as normative documents, the main goal was to harmoniously formulate the worldview of our citizens with the help of artistic images to the ideas of independence. For example, the main tasks set before the decision of August 2, 2017 "on measures for the further development of national cinema"are to preserve and increase the best achievements of Uzbek national cinema, to increase the importance of cinema in the formation of a modern worldview, especially in the formation of a new worldview in the individual, to produce artistically high "As our creators touched on the historical theme, we wanted to take the scope wider, to put the finish high. What mature works have been created in foreign countries that are historically and artistically perfect about such great figures as Spartak, Hannibal, Alexander Macedonsky, Napoleon, Leonardo da Vinci, Beethoven, Leo Tolstoy! Except that our great ones are more than them,but never less. If we want to glorify the memory of our ancestors, on the basis of which we want to glorify the Uzbek name, the name of Uzbekistan, to the whole world, we must first do this through the art of cinema.[38]"

In the field of music, the tasks were also aimed at educating the younger generation in the spirit of patriotism and devotion to the ideas of independence, forming an artistic-aesthetic culture, our rich national-spiritual heritage, creative achievements of the present time, as well as further improving the work of respect, study and assimilation of universal values.

In order to preserve, study, enrich the traditions that have been formed in Uzbekistan since ancient times, to bring and promote the rare masterpieces of our national fine, applied, miniature art to the world, to use them extensively in the minds of our people in order to strengthen the feelings of national pride and pride, independence and loyalty to the motherland, to build an artistic education system According to him, the social security conditions of the members of the Academy of arts are being equated with the social security conditions of the members of the Academy of Sciences of Uzbekistan. Another

---

[38] Mirziyoev Sh.M. The consent of our people is the highest grade given to our activities. - T.: Uzbekistan, Volume 2, 2018. P. 192.

important issue in the draft resolution is the annual allocation of Rs 2 billion to the Ministry of Culture for the purchase of works created by artists and sculptors into state museums" . Art, free from false ideological zugum and transparent tendentiousness, evokes vivid emotions in such young people, serving for the formation and development of their artistic taste and aesthetic culture. Measures and activities aimed at elevating aesthetic culture were aimed at achieving the chanting of humanistic and noble feelings in all types and genres of our art and preventing the creation of works contrary to morality and high spirituality. For example, in order to create favorable conditions for the promotion of monand dances to the inherent Oriental qualities of our nation, rich spirituality, to preserve the art of dancing from the attack of hatti-movements and dresses based on superficial, inappropriate imitation, contrary to the high spirituality and delicate taste of our people, the following tasks were set:

-collecting, enriching, instilling in the minds of our people, especially the younger generation, deep respect and admiration for these invaluable assets in the minds of the Uzbek people attractive dance patterns that have been formed over the centuries and passed down from generation to generation as a unique heritage, raising in them feelings of national spirituality, respect for our values;

- to preserve, advance dance directions in all regions of our country, to create new artistic communities on this basis, to create a modern Uzbek national dance school, which celebrates the spirituality and independence ideas, and gives aesthetic pleasure to our people.

This is how lapar and songs, which have long been common among our people, but have been forgotten or are about to be forgotten by the zamona zayli, seasonal festive celebrations such as "Lola sayli", "red flower", "Navruz", "Mehrjan" were restored.

The "Boysun spring" folk talent show went global and was held annually in the spring anaanly. The development of the years of independence of traditional music, crafts and folk applied art by spreading wide ears is explained by the following results:

- as traditional Uzbek art is passed down from generation to generation over the centuries, in the process it becomes rich and embodies the hopes, ideals and sorrows of folk dreams. These art forms have become the favorite art of the people with their folkness, simplicity, popularity, influence. The use of such opportunities of folk art is important in the spiritual and aesthetic education of young people;

- folk art, with a wide range of artistic and aesthetic and pleasure opportunities, serves as an effective means of forming national consciousness, National thinking, feelings of national pride and pride, and educating a spiritually harmonious generation;

-the spiritual, artistic, aesthetic, educational, philosophical and educational possibilities of folk art, historically composed, began to attach great importance to the formation of Oriental morality and National way of life.

Such spiritual and aesthetic possibilities of folk art were first embodied in the 1997 music festival "taronas of the East" in Samarkand.

In recognition of the tradition of the 12th International Conference of "eastern taronas" by artists from 75makat of the world, President Shavkat Mirziyoev said at the opening of this festival: "well known to all of us, various art and music conferences are held in many continents and regions of the world. The international music festival" taronas of the east " stands out among them for its special place, Fame and status.Because of this festival, the Munavvar koshanas, which today reflect the distant past of the legendary Samarkand, along with the air of the Watcher, charming and charming taranas radiating from this sacred ground, are also encouraging the people of the world. "

Consequently, such festivals, the enjoyment, preservation, advancement, and continuation of the nation's decorative art patterns have been a spiritual factor in the compassion, kindness, harmony, friendship, and creative collaborations between people, peoples, and countries. Our country's tabrigida addressed to the participants of the twelfth World Music Festival" taronas of the East " once again noted that this festival serves as an indispensable tool in realizing the vital need of the world's people for mutual cultural communication in the spirit of every nation, every nation, a long-standing sense of good, beauty and desire for elegance. "For the past pale quarter of a century, the blue domes of Samarkand, how many magical Navos, life-giving tones sounded under the starry sky.The Festival has discovered dozens of famous singers and musicians, unique young talents, bringing wings, energy and inspiration to their flight.[39]"

After independence, the literature and art of our republic began to progress on the basis of such preconceived, consistent, programs, instructions and cares that were raised to the level of a state program. The theater has a special role in elevating the people, in particular, the aesthetic culture of young people. The building of the theater, interior decoration, stage appearance, performance of actors, up to the quality of lighting equipment strongly affect the soul and mind of the viewer. K.S. Stanislavsky did not in vain say that the theater begins where clothes hang. For example, the Uzbek drama Theater glorifies love, goodness and Justice, qualities such as enlightenment and friendship, humanity and kindness, problems through its performances. Vahonki said that " the repertoire of most of our theaters is ideologically-artistically disadvantaged, the performances that have taken their place do not reflect on the breath of today, the serious social problems that make people

---

[39] Mirziyoev Sh.M. The consent of our people is the highest grade given to our activities. - T.: Uzbekistan, Volume 2, 2018. P. 197.

think, excite. Unfortunately, our theaters are more accustomed to showing light-elpi, bachkana works on domestic topics, performances that give a person neither spiritual food nor aesthetic pleasure." Therefore, the Academic drama Theater, revived in a national spirit and modern image, was given the name of the National Academic drama Theater of Uzbekistan. Elegant conditions, spiritual and aesthetic atmosphere were created for thousands of art lovers to watch the colorful performances created in our national theater with admiration and excitement, pleasure and enthusiasm, to think deeply about independence, the beauty of life, the publication of creativity, faith, honor, national pride.

On August 8, 2017, a decision was made" on measures to further develop and improve the activities of the State Conservatory of Uzbekistan". According to the decision, the development of musical art on the basis of the national musical heritage of the Uzbek people and masterpieces of World Music Culture, the development of the best examples of national and universal musical art by our population, first of all, the development of young people on the basis of their cultural level, training personnel for the direction of music, in addition to inviting foreign specialists to our country, the systematic organization of master classes of musicians and educators who achieved high results in our republic in foreign countries, further increasing the creative activity of professors and students of the conservatory and its talented children's academic Lyceum, the transfer of a sanatorium located in the Bostanlyk District of Tashkent region with the name "music retreat" to This comprehensively revealed the importance of youth in raising aesthetic spirituality[40]:

- a person may not be able to write-draw, read, but he will feel the life-giving effect of beautiful melodies, tones and taronas in any situation, in his heart, of course, echoes;

- music, art gives a person strength, spiritual support not only in days of joy, but also in various States, encourages him to live, live, work and enjoy beauty;

- no matter how far from his homeland, a person remembers el-yurt when he meets his national work of Art, close to his heart, even while walking in foreign lands, feelings of

---

[40] Mirziyoev Sh.M. The consent of our people is the highest grade given to our activities. - T.: Uzbekistan, Volume 2, 2018. P. 211.

longing strike in his heart;

- real works of art have a universal language, which will have the property of giving artistic and aesthetic pleasure to all peoples, nations and nationalities without translation.

Art is such an educational, spiritual and educational opportunity and a social miracle of importance. Literature and art have the power to stimulate, inspire, and nurture the qualities of social life and enjoyment of the beauties of nature, as well as the expression of the processes taking place in the consciousness and consciousness of the nation. Literature and art become the pulpit of progressive ideas and goals, especially in a time when there are serious changes in the life of the nation and the country, changes, processes of realization of the identity of the nation, purification and spiritual recovery take place.

In the example style, it is permissible to refer to some poems of the talented poet Muhammad Yusuf. In the poetry of the poet, the folk lesson, his past and future stand in the poetic balance of two shades of Libra. When he recalls the past, he said "to cheer up the spirit of the moms who alla told Alpomish, to remember the

children who put the ladder on the stars, not to pour gaddin, but to know his destiny" " be a people, glue!"exclaims. Therefore, the unity, peace of El is preferable to everything:
The children of Olar el are one after another,
The children of El, who will not be, husband each other.
Be one now, give up the high gadding,
Become people, become people, glue, become people, glue!
(From the poem" become a people, elim").

    The poetry of Muhammad Yusuf is characterized by its simplicity, sincerity, finding a way to the heart of every student, in short, extremely delicate national tone and color. He is a literal independence era poet. Many of his poems would not have seen the face of light at the time of the mustabid regime. The National Colorite in it, the sensations that defined the national mentality, from imperceptible, subtle experiences and passionate lines, of course, no communist ideologies were found. The poet enjoys the fact that in his poetry he is a descendant of the tin-clad Shepherd Muqannayu Temur Malik, Alpomishu Babur, Yassaviu Mashrab, Goh shod, gohghamgin wanders the streets of our history, perceives many things and tries to instill them in the psyche of his contemporaries:

My land, you have broad heavens as well as your heart,
You have sagas that made the star cry.
Zor thy diydoran, beyond thy heavens,
You have desolate fields like gazelles.
Press my face on the packaging of your hand,
My mother-you-ku, my word heavy Apple,
The eyes of the crow closing the birch barbs
You have the Ottomans left in the distance.
Alhazar, alhazar, ming boron alhazar,
Ana, the wearer of the walkers,
Those who are poets who buy the Almighty –
You have scorpions that come out of mehrobing...

The poems of Muhammad Yusuf are full of patriotism, humanity, feelings of national pride, images. Whether he remembers the mysterious, enigmatic, terrible and heartbreaking plates of Mozi, thinks about the village, sister and mother where he was born and grew up, whether he creates poetic lines that are a spiritual bridge between today and the future before his eyes stands the only and holy homeland – the people of Uzbekistan and dear to the soul. For him, there is no secluded homeland in the world from

Uzbekistan, nor a beautiful settlement. Therefore, he proudly sings in the poem "Uzbekistan" the bedapoya of his country to Rome, the tandiri not to get to the most beautiful restaurants in Paris, without belittling the husnu Jamol of other countries, the qaddu qamat.

The dramatic works of Erkin Vohidov, Abdulla Oripov, Muhammad Yusuf, Halima Khudoyberdieva, Aydin Khojieva, Sirojiddin Sayid, Othman Azim, Hayitmat Rasul, Tohir Malik, Erkin Khushvaktov, Dilbar and tilab Mahmudov on the formation of spiritual and aesthetic consciousness of young people, in the development of moral and aesthetic feelings of national pride and patriotism, humanity, or- nomus, Mehru consequence. Therefore, the upbringing of the spiritual culture of the younger generation is considered an urgent task in every society, forming the main link between today and history. The exaltation of the aesthetic heritage of the youth of the society in which we live imposes enormous tasks on literature and art, aimed at artistic expression of the essence and content of the spirituality of independence. Literature and art have been and remain one of the necessary factors in the spiritual-moral and aesthetic education of young people.

Art, in its nature, harmoniously combined with national ideology and national idea, serves a lot in maturing our past, respect for our national self, high confidence in the future, humane feelings. Introducing young people to the world of images of art provides the necessary socio-spiritual ground for an aesthetic culture that leads them to perfection. In the recent past, under the Soviets, on the basis of socialist realism, "works that are far from nationality, fake and false expressions of life landscapes and the beliefs of people, had multiplied like mushrooms that came out after the rain[41]," writes Zhurakul Bakhronov.

As a result, during this period, the main aesthetic characteristics of art that affect a person were deliberately forgotten. His task was also evaluated from the point of view of the execution of the daily requirements that the main idea expresses, alhol, the works created and the personality of the writer-from this point of view.

In the period of independence, the attitude towards our literature was formed in the spirit of new aesthetic principles, works reflecting the free

---

[41] Bakhronov J. The laws by which a person realizes his national identity. - Samarkand: Zarafshan, 1995. P. 112.

themes of young creators, the centuries-old aspirations of our people, the signs experienced, were aimed at showing the subtle aspects of the national, religious, human traditions of our history.

In the process of transition to market economy relations, the issue of aesthetic culture of young people has become a big problem. Some young people, not knowing how to spend their free time, unable to cope with their own desires and desires, cannot find ways to study art, engage in some type of art, lead a life with entrepreneurship. As a result, a gap began to be felt in their spiritual, artistic-aesthetic world. When the social reasons for this were studied, it turned out that, firstly, in theaters there was a decrease in performances that were aesthetically perfect and related to youth life, and secondly, theaters were located mainly in cities and the regular non-functioning of rural cinemas, and thirdly, due to the conditions of a market economy, the attention to moral and aesthetic education of The social and spiritual reasons for this phenomenon were explained by Shavkat

Mirziyoev: [42] "at the moment, there are practically no modern infrastructure networks for conducting educational and educational events in the harsh rural areas. For example, in the districts of Bakhmal, Mirzaabad, Khovos, Middle Chirchik, parks for young people, cinemas do not exist at all" indicate that the work that should be done has not yet been completed.

At a time when the construction of the current democratic society has spread wide ears, every worker, servant, peasant, entrepreneur, businessman, farmer, intellectual should not forget to enjoy art and literature, in addition to introducing knowledge, skills of expertise to Life, Production. Only then does the social activity of a person become more active. Thanks to the implementation of this principle, joyarda is leading to the emergence of many circles of artistic amateurs, the restoration, development of our historical heritage, traditions. The fact that young people are engaged in some type of art in their free time, in addition to production, not only increases their artistic and aesthetic culture, but also positively affects their labor efficiency.

---

[42] Mirziyoev Sh.M. The consent of our people is the highest grade given to our activities. - T.: Uzbekistan, Volume 2, 2018. P. 513.

Today, artistic amateur circles, folk ensembles, folk theaters are organized in every Enterprise, factory, company farms and other labor communities, which are enriched with a colorful repertoire, and these amateurs show their art on stages, in houses of culture, in clubs. An example of this is the circle of folk singing and dancing artistic amateurs "five claps", organized under the Urgut District of the Samarkand region.

In the occurrence of fundamental changes in the spiritual and aesthetic culture of our youth, the care of professional artists operating in the regions of our republic in teaching art secrets to artistic amateur communities is of great importance. The good establishment of such artistic creative cooperation has become one of the factors of the rise of the aesthetic culture of our people.

Professional political figures are greatly helped by the fact that local youth bring a universal spiritual culture into the pleasure activities, which are imbued with national values, with our heritage, to demonstrate the more serjilo facets of our national art. Such creative cooperation is shaping and developing the intellectual level, worldview of young people on the basis of national and universal values. Such a spiritual and aesthetic culture becomes a universal property and becomes a symbol of applause and admonition. "As the eastern sages say,"the greatest wealth is intelligence and science, the greatest inheritance is good upbringing, the greatest poverty is ignorance[43]"!

Therefore, for all of us, mastering modern knowledge, becoming truly enlightened and the owner of a high culture should become a continuous vital need.

To achieve progress, it is necessary and necessary for us to master digital knowledge and modern information technology. This gives us the opportunity to follow the shortest path of ascent. After all, today Information Technology is penetrating into all spheres of the world,[44] " President Sh.M.Mirziyoev.

As a result of the development of Science and technology at the beginning of the 21st century, many films shown on television are created directly on the basis of computer

---

[43] Mirziyoev Sh.M. Appeal to the people of Uzbekistan. Newspaper "People's word", 2020, 25yanvar.
[44] Mirziyoev Sh.M. The consent of our people is the highest grade given to our activities. - T.: Uzbekistan, Volume 2, 2018. P. 202.

technology. Therefore, instead of spiritual values such as nationalism,patriotism, humanity, grandeur, cinema and discs associated with events such as violence, aggression, hypocrisy, immorality are shown in large numbers in the cinema that is being created. Such works undermine the formation of a pure and delightful aesthetic culture of a person. Our President Sh.M.As Mirziyoev noted: "it is about the need to set an example for others, above all for our youth, with artistic manners, their manners, their culture of dress, their treatment. The cheerful singer remembers the once charming songs of Sanobar Rakhmonova, which the audience still misses now. This artist was an example of how many of our girls, creating an image, a genuine image of an iboli, imaginary, real Uzbek girl, both on the TV channel and on the stage. Unfortunately, some clips that are being made on television today could not be watched in the company of Family, Children. When you see young people dressed in open-cut clothes, in every movement of which an imitation of the West is felt, you will think that these are also our children, representatives of our nation. Of course, it is natural that such problems also plague our master creators, who consider art sacred."

Therefore, in a period of intense struggle for spiritual and moral purification, high aesthetic culture in the Republic of Uzbekistan, it is necessary not to show films that are considered foreign to the traditions of our people, without delusions, upbringing, stigmatizing human honor, harming the upbringing of young people, but, on the contrary, the most beautiful and instructive features, habits,, on the interpretation of the concepts and lifestyle, the Cabinet of Ministers Resolution No. 502 of July 17, 2017 "on measures to be implemented to switch to digital TV and stop terrestrial analog TV broadcasts" was announced. Measures have been taken to increase all sources, means, including National Education on television and radio, shows and broadcasts on national aesthetic culture, encouraging young people to have beautiful morals, spiritual maturity in their attitudes towards life and art.

In the formation of aesthetic culture, in addition to literature, theater, cinema and television, which are associated with the national mentality and socio-philosophical ideas, there are also examples of such artistic creation, which, although not directly carrying the ideological burden, play a huge role in the formation of folk artistic and aesthetic culture with its national-spiritual roots, significance. For example, the folk art of practical decoration, deeply embedded in the way of life of our nation, has found a new bleakness in the process of democratization and liberalization of our spiritual activities due to independence.

The history of such a delicate and unique art is very long and gloomy, like the history and fate of the people. This art is an example of the potential of creativity, creativity of the people. Not only " Egyptian pyramids that have fascinated the world for several centuries, Oqsaroy in Shahrisabz, Bibikhonim in Samarkand, a set of madrasas in Registan Square, the Tojmahal monument, the Eiffel Tower, many masterpieces of art and culture-all are examples of such creativity. Such miracles are reflected in our cultural heritage, unique monuments in Khiva, Bukhara, traditions and traditions based on high morality in our works of classical art.[45]"

In the years of independence, this traditional art form has been gaining renewed vigor as a material and spiritual wealth that

---

[45] The idea of national independence. - T.: Acadymia, 2005. P. 52.

adorns the lifestyle of the people, attracting the attention of the peoples of the world. An example of this is that carving, ganching, wood polishing were in full swing. There are many examples of the rise of folk aesthetic culture. By the time, the popularization of art samples has expanded in form and possibilities. Classical songs written on tapes, songs, pop songs and videos and TV movies were able to be viewed, chanted, enjoyed wherever and whenever anyone wanted. The computer further expanded this capability.

In the conditions of market relations, the number of traders with video shows, feature films written on cassettes, songs opened in the cities and villages of our republic has become much more. But in this area, too, it is necessary to operate within the framework of our national spirituality. Because in these samples of" popular culture", plaques, melodies, songs are also promoted, which are contrary to Oriental morality, such as betrayal, immorality. Such negative situations are also caused by the neglect of employees working in some spirituality and educational centers.

So, without strengthening the role of literature and art in the education of the aesthetic culture of the individual, the spiritual life of independence cannot be formed as a whole system. The national aesthetic thinking of young people, considered a great social force in the process of reforming the spiritual life of the independence period on the basis of the demand for market relations, cannot be built on the basis of the laws of beauty, and the intended goal – civil society. Therefore, during the period of independence, when a new thinking and worldview of people is being formed, based on the construction of a new society and a new way of living, the social status and functions of national literature and art change. Through the free expression of the problems of reform processes and prospects in our country by the people of creativity, the opportunity and responsibility of raising the people, especially young people, the artistic and aesthetic culture of the individual is enhanced.

The political, economic, and spiritual reforms carried out in our country required literature and art, which monandically instilled in the minds of young people the spirit of our history, national identity, tradition and heritage, the spiritual and ideological essence of modern reforms and could educate them in the spirit of patriotism, hard work and Oriental morality, aesthetic culture, soon examples of such artistic creativity appeared. For this, a number of decrees and decisions of the president and Cabinet of Ministers of the Republic of Uzbekistan were announced, in all of which it was noted to create all the conditions for free activities for creators and to form a harmonious generation, to increase the role and importance of literature and art in raising its aesthetic culture.

The importance of literature and art in social life and in personality spirituality is great. In a person who is closely acquainted with artistic creativity, glorious experiences, bright intentions, feelings of initiative, creativity are matured. Such a high mood, no matter in which area a person works, motivates him to social activity. Aesthetic culture leads young people to spiritual purification, independence ideas, pride in results and ideals.

Chapter Two. Features of the formation of aesthetic culture in the Uzbek mentality in the process of globalization

2.1§. Distinctive features in the formation of aesthetic culture in the era of globalization

Globalization has always ensured the diversity of human historical development, cultural heritage, social order and ideology. This process began to show its new appearance even in the formation of the aesthetic culture of the individual in Uzbekistan during the years of independence. Particular attention is required to pay special attention to the issues of educating the younger generation, which will be brought up in the family on the basis of high aesthetic ideals, ensuring that they will develop into a comprehensively mature person in the system of continuing education. Providing care for young families, creating conditions for women's marriage and work, Maternal Protection and activation of their activities in state and public organizations are the main directions of this process.

Globalization, which plays a special role in the rapid development of the process of social development, is gaining new meaning and meaning in the aesthetic culture of each state, people, nation or individual. In the development of society, "just as every social phenomenon has its positive and negative side, the process of globalization is no exception. At the moment, its incredibly sharp and comprehensive effect can be seen, felt in almost all areas. In particular, the strengthening of integration and cooperation between states and peoples, the emergence of foreign investments, capital and goods, facilities for the free movement of the labor force, the creation of many new jobs, the rapid spread of modern communication and information technology, achievements of Science, the harmonization of various values on a universal basis, a new qualitative occupation of inter-civilizational Dialogue, an increase in In such a situation, only a person who has firmly established his self, national idea and ideology will introduce modernity into an everyday lifestyle to the level of aesthetic culture, ready for globalization, without the separation of the past from heritage and values[46].

The development strategy of Uzbekistan has become one of the urgent tasks of our society to comprehensively explain the goals of the Uzbek people for the creation of a great state, the essence of the National idea to the general public, to make the true essence and content of the globalization process clear and clear in the role of the individual in aesthetic culture.

In the context of globalization, the rational use of effective methods and means of covering all spheres of the life of society, education, propaganda and propaganda is assumed in the absorption of the National idea into the hearts of each individual, in particular our people. Today, it is known to everyone that globalization is associated with our social life, especially since our material and spiritual wealth has great importance in the prosperity of society.

The role of social consciousness today in the aesthetic culture of an individual is a natural process in which he manifests himself in connection with society. This, in turn, serves to form a new thinking, a new worldview, a new

---

[46] Karimov I.A. High spirituality is an invincible force. - T.: Spirituality, 2008. P. 111-112.

ideological immunity. In the context of globalization, this process should be robust, that is, continuous "with the individual's self-expression, life goals, ties between the state and society with his place in society.[47]"

On the basis of such interaction were the high spirituality of our people, their aesthetic culture, moral and religious views, which have become richer and more established over the centuries. And the globalization process is coming to the field as a force that threatens our past heritage and values. Because globalization, on the one hand, positively affects the development of personality and society, and on the other, with its negative image, threatens all of humanity. In later years," the effect of this process on national-spiritual life, on the absorption of moral values, customs and traditions, is developing especially intensely[48]". From such a situation, each of us should be alert today, to competently protect the masterpieces of spirituality that have been developing in our

---

[47] Musaev F. Philosophical and legal foundations of the construction of a democratic legal state and civil society in Uzbekistan. Author of a doctoral dissertation. - T.: 2008. P. 17.
[48] Otamuratov S. Globalization and nation. - T.: New century generation, 2008. P. 42.

people for centuries.

In relation to changes in all areas of social consciousness, it is necessary for each individual to feel deeply how globalization affects, to be able to find an answer to any harmful aspects of it from the point of view of aesthetic culture.

It is necessary to understand to what extent the power to influence the true causes and essences of the emergence of any new product on the world political scenes, and, moreover, the progress of tomorrow, to be aware of the aspects that threaten the security of our society.

The fact that the negative impact of a large empire in the 20th century on the fate of the nation and the elates caused the emergence of such situations is well understood today by the states that have achieved independence. In a time when they seek to restore their national values and history, it is not up to us to directly accept the new aesthetic values that seek to poison the mind of the younger generation, while pampering the spirit of the times in themselves. Therefore, we are all always aware of the sphere of influence of the developed countries on Globalization, from their gradually negative aspects of the consciousness and psyche of the individual, from their aesthetic cultures, which are entering on the basis of "mass culture[49]", it is a matter of fear. It is advisable to carefully use the progress that seeks to penetrate into the lifestyle, spirituality, aesthetic culture of our people with its products, reflecting such situations. Because, through this psyche and culture, the possibility of achieving progress in each area on the basis of striving to acquire the consciousness of an individual becomes wider. Their "goal of action is also very great, that is, the undeniable fact that it consists in having a great benefit, gaining the economy and material resources of one country or another, acquiring their national spirituality, instilling their traditions, traditions, moral values in the minds and hearts of others, depriving another nation of its spiritual poverty, self-esteem by their implementation[50]".

Today's globalization conditions demand that the aesthetic culture of the individual be perfect and Lush in every way. This is due to the fact that the changes taking place in society do not directly give anyone a chance to deviate from

---

[49] Utkin A.I. Globalization: prosess I osmislenia. –M.: Logos, 2002.- s.6

[50] Let's preserve our greatest wealth – peace and stability. - T.: Acadymia, 2006. P. 119.

globalization, but those who say that I avoid it are more and more caught in his net. A person's passion for information, aesthetic tastes and experiences are leading to this situation without worrying about it. In the process of Social Development, world globalization is manifested as a significant structural aspect of the formation of the modern technotron, informational civilization. [51] Global informational exchange creates a completely different situation in the formation of patriotism from the conditions of the previous time, since first a person was developed in each country, mainly under the influence of the Information System formed by his state, nationality, homeland, now a person is formed on a global scale under the decisive influence of the flow of information created by

At present, globalization on the basis of the information system threatens to change the aesthetic culture of our people, in particular, national and universal values, traditions, rituals and Customs in different ways. The reason for this is that globalization is changing the ideological landscape of the world, giving rise to

---

[51] Fayziev S., Normatov K. Terrorism and youth: problem, solutions. - T.: Publishing house of the Institute of philosophy and Law, 2007. P. 52.

New-new ideas and views. "The Global community is changing the world before our eyes with radically different aspects from previous scientific discoveries and revolutions. The speed and depth of the changes that are taking place require human talent and humanity to adapt side by side, to determine the direction of the changes that are taking place, to coordinate their consciousness with necessity. [52] " As a result, humanity strives to look after its favorable aesthetic environment for itself. Each individual, trying to assimilate the Social Beauty and healthy mental environment of globalization, falls into a space that, without realizing it, negatively affects the national heritage and aesthetic culture.

Such cases show their colorful image in the new century more on the issue of religious extremism and terrorism. On the basis of globalization, terrorism manifests its landscape, masked by ugliness and Abyss, under the slogan "color revolutions". As a result of this, some forces threaten the fate and future of the peoples and pay off their long-standing national values. involving many as their"puppets" in political

---

[52] Let's preserve our greatest wealth – peace and stability. - T.: Acadymia, 2006. P. 112.

games. The resulting "color revolutions" are aimed at reducing the culture and morale of the people of Georgia, Ukraine, Kyrgyzstan. Innocent people are shortening their lives. If, in the interests of these uncivilized and savages, your mouth was anointed once, and you were brought into the trap of extremism and terrorism, then you cannot get rid of this web of evil alive. You will become a bamisoli doll in their hands. They play when it is necessary, they wander when it is necessary, and when it is necessary–they blow it up by making a bomb[53]".

To do this, we need to consistently establish a healthy lifestyle and life in our society, harmonizing each individual primarily with the spirit and feelings of humanity, and to mature our spiritual and educational activities on the basis of the world of beauty. Only then will we be able to hit an ax at the root of the unclean plans of people who, with such an original image in our society, aim for the abyss. On a global scale, "it is not only to realize that at the moment it is impossible to remain a passive observer in relation to international terrorism, aggression, threats and

---

[53] Mirziyoev Sh.M. The intention is that the work of ulughalq is also great, the life of the light, and the future will be prosperous. - Tashkent: Uzbekistan, P. 2019.63.

attacks, but also to actively conduct both practical-organizational and spiritual-educational, propaganda work against it, but in this struggle every citizen, especially young people, manifests their desire to take an active part [54]". The formation of such a social environment directly in society, enriching individual pleasure relations with new artistic and aesthetic ideas, serves as one of the main tools in combating terrorism and religious fanaticism.

Some evil ideas that embody the essence of terrorism are developing today as a system of dissemination of information in all countries of the world. The fact that this information has become the most terrible scourge serves to confuse peoples with their aesthetic cultures. In such a complex situation, "this situation, which poses a great threat to the lives of millions of people living with their hard work, joy, peace and security, can be called, in a sense, "informational terror". The consequence of this upheaval, the terrible essence of which many still do not know and realize, is no less than that of those who enter the life of the terrorist, whose lives are being

---

[54] Mirziyoev Sh.M. The consent of our people is the highest grade given to our activities. - T.: Uzbekistan, Volume 2, 2018. P. 496

claimed by thousands of innocent people in different parts of the Earth.[55]"

Some individuals of our people, who have long been practicing Islam, sometimes fall under the surface of the forces operating under the guise of religious fanaticism. It is a pity that we do not forget that these cases are a threat to the spirituality and culture of our country, which is aimed directly at the development of our country, tomorrow. "For the first time, the law on the state security service of the Republic of Uzbekistan was adopted, which made it the task of a newly created special office to reliably protect the interests of the state from internal and external threats.

In today's alarming time, when the danger of extremism and terrorism, encroachments on the constitutional system and economy of our country are maintained, it is necessary that brave and brave soldiers and officers of the state security service will fight uncompromising against any destructive forces and be a solid shield under the protection of our homeland.[56]"

---

[55] A free and prosperous O'ayot cannot be built without high morale. - T.: Uzbekistan, 2006. P. 16.
[56] Karimov I.A. High spirituality is an invincible force. - Tashkent: Spirituality, 2008. Pp. 13-14.

The spiritual threats posed to the fate and prospects of peoples as a product of global globalization are mainly associated with the transformation of the aesthetic culture of the individual. Such menaces are looking for reforms aimed at making their material and spiritual culture in a superficially beautiful and attractive appearance, an example for others, and, in fact, a bottleneck with its inner essence. Today we often see from the media and the internet that such aesthetic activity is also present in developed countries of the world, in particular, the long-standing aesthetic cultures of such countries as the United States, England, France, Germany, Norway are leading to a sad situation. At the moment, the world "is rapidly changing, the world is facing humanity, opening new horizons and opportunities in front of young people, as well as exposing them to various evil dangers that have not been seen before. As many as there are threats such as religious extremism, terrorism, drugs, human trafficking, illegal migration, "mass culture[57]", which bring severe calamities to the heads of families, countries, mercenary forces

---

[57] Fayziev S., Normatov K. Terrorism and heresy: a riddle, heresy. – T.: Philosophy and Law Publishing Institute, 2007, 55-bet.

have not yet fully formed the mind of children against their parents, their homeland and take their lives. Therefore, we-parents, mentor-mentors, the public, the neighborhood-further increase vigilance and alertness in this matter and, as our great-enlightened grandfather Abdurauf Fitrat said, We need to deeply understand that this world is really becoming a field of struggle, and a healthy body, sharp mind and good morality is becoming the weapon of this struggle, and work on this

In our society, it is an urgent issue to establish a greater impact of globalization on the aesthetic culture of the individual on the basis of more nationalism and age-old values. In order to save our nation from such storms, we must first preserve our religion as a black eye, strengthen our faith and faith, and instill our morals and Customs in the minds and hearts of every citizen on the basis of feelings of humanity and aesthetic ideals.

In our country, serious attention is paid to these issues, the buildings of the "youth center", which serve for the system of continuing education in all regions of the Republic, aimed at the formation of a high aesthetic culture, in which thousands of our youth are strengthening their feelings of confidence in the future with our national heritage and ceremonies. In particular, in the center of " spirituality and enlightenment "on the campus" youth", located in the capital of our country, a club" nafosat "is organized, where special attention is paid to the preparation of girls for life, the formation of their aesthetic taste, especially the issues of dress culture[58].

Globalization, which has a deeper and deeper impact on the human mind, should at the same time not disdain every member of society, be aware of the various visible freedoms embedded in the way of life of countries and peoples of the world, perfectly assimilate the thoughtful vessels of our national values and Ma'anavit so as not to make themselves dependent on others. The development of aesthetic immunity from "ideological, ideological and informational attacks aimed at the goal of literally living as a free person, to exclude his spiritual world," from the various flow of information that is rapidly entering darkor. On the basis of aesthetic immunity, an individual's perception of reality, concepts, aesthetic ideals

---

[58] Normatov K., Kyrgyzbaev A. Tashkent City. –T.: 2007. 4-bet.

become more viable and beautiful.

In the field of religion, which today is the most delicate and complex, it should first be borne in mind that religion is one of the pillars of spirituality and culture, in all times the National idea and ideology develop harmoniously with religious views. Religion, in its essence, instills the ideas of national ideology in the hearts and minds of our compatriots through such noble feelings as purity, kindness. The formation of a healthy and moderate attitude towards our sacred religion is the most important ideological task in this regard.

Therefore, at a high level, the formation of an aesthetic culture of the individual, that is, "a modern person harmonizes national, religious and Universal – secular values in his secular worldview and practical position. He cannot allow ecclesiastical incontinence, while showing high respect for religious values. That is, recognizing and respecting the sacred values that the modern man is the product of the medieval way of life, understandable only to the man of that time, it is an objective necessity not to return to the values of medieval life, worldview, values, but to adapt to the values of high technologies, universal and democratic progress."

Religious traditions, rituals and holidays that have been formed and developed over the centuries, passed down from generation to generation as an invaluable legacy, also occupy an important place in the absorption of aesthetic culture into the consciousness of the individual. In particular, the Uzbek people "rule and arcons in their lives, ancient traditions and values, the contribution of this land to Islamic civilization and culture for centuries, what high-minded people, great Ulama lived here, and the scientific and spiritual heritage left by them" greatly contribute to the prosperity of the aesthetic culture of the entire Muslim world.

Today in our country, religion has become an important factor in the development of our society, as a spiritual and ideological principle in shaping the aesthetic culture of the individual. The main reasons for this are the increasing and strengthening of the role of different religions in our society and their tolerance for each other.

The essence of this aesthetic culture is that it has long been formed in the minds and hearts of our people and has been practiced in our homeland. This religion manifests a complex harmonic development of a person's philosophical, natural, moral, historical, artistic, spiritual and aesthetic views.

The aesthetic culture of the individual means that people with diverse religious beliefs live together and in harmony in the path of noble ideas and intentions on the same floor, in the same Homeland.

Also, aesthetic culture expresses that in society, people of different religions and different religions are in a Commonwealth relationship, while at the same time, regardless of people's beliefs, they cooperate in the path of a common goal. In particular, if this issue is considered in relation to the religion of Islam, then we can be sure that this idea came from the essence of this religion. The Qur'an says in the "Hujorot" of Karim: "O mankind, we have created you from a man and a woman, and meet each other, and be friends and brothers, and we have made you different peoples, tribes, elates, and whoever acts in piety is the most respected person in the presence of Allah. Or, the Prophet said,"Whoever hurts the people of other religions will hurt me."

History itself raised our people in the spirit of the need to treat all religions with pleasure, and therefore aesthetic culture was absorbed into their blood and soul.

Since the ancient past, aesthetic culture has been supported on the territory of our motherland among various religions or their representatives. For example, coins minted during the Kushan dynasty featured a Buddha-a symbol of the official religion of the state-on one side, while the other side featured a symbol of another religion. Arab historians write that when Islam came into Bukhara, religious types such as Buddhism, Zoroastrianism, Christianity, Monianism and shamanism were practiced at the same time, and their adherents lived in harmony, harmony with each other. At some point in time, Termez had a place of Worship, Church, hearth, and kalisos of Buddhism, Zoroastrianism, monism, Christianity, and Judaism. All this shows that people are united in the path of prosperity of the motherland, striving for a high aesthetic culture.

Historically it is known that the MA'mun Academy employed great Christian religious scholars such as Abul Khair Hammor with Abu Sahl the Christian. It is noteworthy that the Christian Scientist Abu Sahl was the second teacher of the Christian Beruni after Ibn Iraq, and

Amir Tumur sent a priest of the Sultanian church (Azerbaijan)to Europe as his chief ambassador. Also during the reign of Zahiddin Muhammad as king of Beaver, India was settled by peoples of various religions and sects. The fact that Beaver Mirza was a wise king has clearly found its expression in the correct way of his mutual pleasure attitude of these different religions. In particular, in a letter to his son Camron Mirza, he argues that an aesthetic culture should be strengthened in the state and condemns any contradictions that arise between different religions and religious currents, and considers it heretical. Our greatness considered this idea not only a priority idea of state policy, but at the same time applied it to the work of instructive practical creativity. For example, at that time in India built such a majestic temple that from one door Muslims, one-Christians, the other- representatives of other religions could freely enter and freely fulfill their prayers. Akmal Saidov believes that for the character of our fervent ancestors-good manners such as hayo, contentment, Rizo, thanks, patience, repentance, diligence, humility, tolerance, jumardism, prudence, kindness, consequence, dishonesty, justice-were typical.

Nowadays, it is becoming extremely important that all spheres and aspects of social life are more and more firmly connected with the globalization process, spiritual and ideological threats and conflicts on a global scale increase and escalate, the struggle to occupy the minds and hearts of every person intensifies, political and religious extremists and terrorists continue to practice aesthetic culture effectively in every state.

If in society the aesthetic culture of a person is violated and replaced by the idea of religious tolerance, then on the scale of one country there is a phenomenon of discord and war-animosity, both between representatives of different nationalities and nationalities and between states. As an example of this, to some extent, on the scale of the current States of Lebanon, Afghanistan and Iraq, we can get the sad events and events that took place in the relations between India and Pakistan, Armenia and Azerbaijan.

When the fight against religion in one country is conducted at the level of public policy, then as the role and role of different religions in society shrinks and decreases, the influence of people on culture also slows down. Such a spiritual and mental state that arises in the country, instead of friendly and benevolent pleasure relations between members of society, people of different nationalities and nationalities, religions, is formed by deep-rooted mistrust, alienation, cruelty and other unpleasant feelings and attitudes. Such relations are the basis for the origin of discord and quarrels, unnecessary bloodshed, other-other tragedies among various nationalities and elates in society, representatives of religion. It is known to all that such cases were observed during the time of the former Soviet state.

After independence in Uzbekistan, the political forces of some states were eager to establish a unified Caliphate State on the territory of Central Asia, based on Islam. The original purpose of these forces, masking Islam, was to destroy the sovereign states in the area and instead pursue their own political and ideological goals. But on the basis of the rational policies of our country, wide opportunities have been implemented in our republic to treat religion from an aesthetic point of view, to glorify Islam, the basis of our long-standing values, to the world. As a result of this, the contributions of our great ancestors to religion were glorified and their birth and blessed names were immortalized. Imam al-Bukhari's name was glorified and the Imam al-Bukhari shrine and Imam al-Bukhari International Center were built in Payariq District of Samarkand region. In addition, the names of Bahawuddin Naqshband, Imam al-Moturudi, az-Zamakhshari, at-Termiziy and dozens of our religious scribes were immortalized.

Such extensive work has attracted all Muslim states worldwide. The outstanding achievements of our people towards the prosperity of the Islamic religion were studied by the International Islamic Organization for Education, Science and culture, AYSESCO, which declared the city of Tashkent in 2007 and Bukhara in 2020 as the "capital of Islamic culture". This, in turn, testifies to the fact that in our country special attention is paid to the harmony of personality and religion, and aesthetic culture is based on long-standing and national values.

At present, aesthetic culture has deep roots in political, economic, legal, spiritual, religious, moral, aesthetic and other aspects of social life, which is of paramount importance in society. The more aesthetic culture is strengthened in society, the easier it is to instill so many national values, Ana'anas, traditions and rituals in the minds and hearts of people.

Another important reason why religion and aesthetic culture are so important in our country is that our homeland is a multi-ethnic and religious state, in which more than 2,200 religious organizations are now practiced. There are 16 religious denominations in operation, 2,040 mosques, 163 Christian churches, 7 Jewish communities, 7 Baha'i communities, 2 Krishna Consciousness societies and 15 religious institutions (Tashkent Islamic Academy, Tashkent Islamic Institute, Imam al Bukhari International Training Center, 10 madrasas and 1 Orthodox and 1 Full Gospel Christian seminary) are registered in the state. In all this, special attention is paid to the place of the individual in society, and a new modern aesthetic worldview is put forward.

Today, it is necessary to make more complete use of the unifying features of our traditions and traditions of society.

We witness that Uzbekistan is experiencing

a period of national awakening in the process of independent development, the conflict between goodness and evil is growing in the world at a time when our cultural heritage, national traditions, values are being restored.

Therefore, any aesthetic culture will be viable, influential only if it takes into account the national traditions and lifestyle of the spiritual spiritual needs of the people. At the same time, in the process of globalization, the task of the individual to carry out reforms for the formation of a new aesthetic culture is in our focus on the basis of a national idea.

Our knowledge of the history of our ancestors and knowledge of the ideas and history of the peoples of the world are powerful means of forming a sense of respect for the National idea in the minds of every citizen. The motherland is a great adoration for each of us, on the basis of which ideological struggles in the system of informed society and state construction, various cultural and educational ties play a huge role in the increase in the role and importance of feelings of striving for beauty, enjoying life in the aesthetic culture of the individual.

As a result of the work carried out in this

area, we need to instill in the consciousness of the individual not only that nature, the state, society are free from various dangers, to live, to leave offspring, but also to unite with others, have high taste and wisdom, strive to build a free and prosperous homeland, cooperate and achieve the goals pursued.

In Uzbekistan, the strengthening of interaction with the world community requires a new reflection and awareness in social life. This process in itself provided ample opportunities for the harmony of the lifestyle and worldview of our people with modern ideas. In the minds of citizens, along with national values, a new-looking lifestyle began to form. The process of integralization that arose between Farb culture and Eastern culture began to cause the assimilation and transformation of human consciousness in different regions and regions in different manifestations (both positively and negatively).

In a way of living that changes from day to day in society, different images directly affect the mind that is forming healthy, creating the globalization of thoughts.

Philosopher Q.Khonnazarov believes that "

due to globalization, the process of becoming a universal market of the whole world is accelerating and accelerating every year. It emphasizes that in order to solve various problems and issues of work, trade, economic, political and others in the market at a high pace in the spirit of the times, it is required to "find a language" with representatives of the opposing side, to come to a "general decision""1 will give rise to tests. Taken from the point of view of this opinion, the globalization process gradually penetrates into the national values, traditions and Ana'anas of each people as a negative influence on the healthy lifestyle that is taking shape in society.

It is a social issue to strive to live together with today's modern ideas, to build confidence and faith in the impartiality of thoughts and views in our healthy lifestyle, which are interpreted differently, without losing the National thinking that all our citizens have historically held strong beliefs in a time when the globalization process that is taking place in the world's political

To achieve that the globalization process does not adversely affect our national values, we must all work with caution and caution. Because our nationality, which has been inherited by the future generation for centuries without suffering, is recognized today by the peoples of the whole world.

In teaching their youth in a healthy culture and lifestyle in society, it is advisable to decide on the succession between history and today. It is important to mature every citizen in the spirit of a national idea, to improve the skill of personal upbringing in the family is of positive importance.

The formation of a healthy lifestyle of citizens in society is carried out on the basis of various conditions. One of these is manifested in the formation of an attitude towards the environment in the psyche of nationalism, preservation of ancestral heritage, mutual sincerity, commitment to values.

The Uzbek people have their rich philosophical and aesthetic heritage. Our lifestyle depends on this heritage, that is, it is developing in connection with Oriental national upbringing. Also, the content of the verses of Karim, Hadith Sharifs, great alloma and the treasure of the precious rare books of our philosophers, which brought the world of sophistication to the young generation, is aimed at improving not only the healthy social environment in Uzbekistan, but also the kindness among the peoples of the world. Today, the process of globalization in Uzbekistan, which has been calling the World Day by day with its prestige and reputation, has made the modern and national ideology a requirement of the era for creating only positive interests, as well as a perfect marriage for the future. In fact, the implementation of this very delicate and bold work requires the children of the entire Uzbek people to be patient, diligent, aspiring. Such qualities as faith in our children, national pride, patriotism and humanity directly show their influence on the prosperity of independent Uzbekistan.

Today, the peculiarities of the aesthetic culture of a person "also depend on the potential of the nation's social, economic, political, spiritual-spiritual accustomed to the processes of world globalization.[59]" This connection, in turn, requires that globalization in society is comprehensive, that each individual uses it wisely, that the unique aspects of our lifestyle are approached with high respect and feelings of

---

[59] Mirziyoev Sh.M. The intention is that the work of ulughalq is also great, the life of the light, and the future will be prosperous. - Tashkent: Uzbekistan, P. 2019.355.

humanity.

Each individual creates in the context of globalization a delightful relationship of social progress through his spiritual maturation and aesthetic culture. At the time of this delightful relationship, such as deep assimilation and awareness of the long-standing values of our people, emotional and delightful perception of reality, thoughtful observation of the national and universal characteristics of our history become an urgent problem. Their solution, on the other hand, continues to develop in the highest spiritual-moral and artistic-aesthetic views of the individual.

In conclusion, in the process of globalization, the task of ensuring the continuity of the aesthetic culture of the individual with the National idea, ensuring that the reforms carried out are productive and beneficial for each member of society, as well as realizing the eternity of enjoying modern achievements, harmonizing nationalism with commonality, is the force calling the people of Uzbekistan towards noble goals under

2.2§. Issues of harmonization of aesthetic culture with valeoesthetic education in the Uzbek mentality

The globalization of the world requires a radical reform of the educational process of each country and the harmonization of the aesthetic culture of the individual with modern valeoesthetic education. In all areas of social life, the adaptation of the aesthetic culture of the individual and society to globalization, in the process of moretheoestetics, has put the creation of opportunities for the stabilization of the Serbian system with perfect national values on the field as an urgent problem today. As a result, today, the head of our state, Shavkat Mirziyoyev, in his speeches and lectures, set out to find a solution to this extremely serious and untenable problem.

Reflecting on the relevance of ideological and spiritual education on the basis of "national revival – national rise" in the new society, the head of the country says that "it is especially important to radically improve the quality and level of educational processes on the basis of modern requirements, create decent working conditions for our hardworking teachers, all dedicated people operating in this area, Indeed, valeoesthetic upbringing is a huge source of strength, an important system of the development of society, which brings up a person as an active person.

The development of the basis of valeoesthetic education in society on the basis of our rich past heritage, invaluable material and spiritual resources of our ancestors, the creation of an educational system corresponding to the world template has become an urgent issue. Because in the development of our future tomorrow "it is necessary to introduce our children into a new way of thinking, with high human feelings, to continuously develop in them the ability to think independently and creatively.

I am sure that, regardless of nationality, language and religion, you, dear teachers and coaches of Uzbekistan, who work diligently to love and ardently educate each child as their own child and make them perfect people, will definitely fulfill these duties with honor." These people are our young people today, who are able to demonstrate the prosperous life and beautiful culture of our society, national values and great history to the whole world in the context of Tapestry, and, if necessary, to bring the prospect of their country to high heights. For our young people, it is necessary that, above all, every family, neighborhood, social organization, various foundations and associations of our society be aware of the basics of valeoesthetic education, prepare the ground for their upbringing as an aesthetically cultured person, be taken as both a responsibility and a main goal. In all these places,[60] "serious changes are also being made in the system of Science and education, taking into account the demand of today's era, the desires and desires of our people. The school education system has been radically changed and 11 years of general secondary education is being revived. New higher education institutions, scientific and creative centers are being established in a number of regions of our country. Admission quotas for higher education institutions were significantly increased. Correspondence and evening forms of higher education are being restored. Also, one of the issues that makes us think the most about this is the radical reform of the preschool education

---

[60] Mirziyoev Sh.M. The consent of our people is the highest grade given to our activities. - T.: Uzbekistan, Volume 2, 2018. P. 228.

system. Our goal is to fully integrate kindergarten-age children in our country into such educational institutions in the next 3-4 years, and we will definitely achieve this."

The Uzbek mentality is inspired by such energetic pleasure relationships that make each young generation mature as individuals who serve the fate and prospects of society, penetrate into the global environment with a new life. In society, valeoesthetics, the harmonization of Austria with aesthetic culture at the time of pleasure relations, forms the atmosphere of Social Beauty and the spiritual world of high humanity.

The rise of the aesthetic culture of the individual in the period of the establishment of a new Uzbekistan is directly reflected in the statement: "all our laws and decisions, plans and programs are aimed at updating and modernizing our country, deepening economic reforms, improving the activities of the state power and management system, law enforcement, health, education, increasing the combat potential of our armed forces – all this

At the moment, each people and each era will have their own artistic and aesthetic values and lifestyle, which will acquire a characteristic feature, express the valeoesthetic upbringing of the period. The division of these diverse cultures into species in turn plays a special role for each nation. The aesthetic culture of the individual also tries to feed on national spirituality in this case. Because as long as the world is full of nations and peoples, the values of each of them that are not the same as the others become richer in the process of globalization. "If all people on Earth speak the same language, they have the same traditions,traditions, values, religion, or reflect Family, Child Education, domestic life and a number of other material and spiritual factors in the same way, there was no need for them to live talpinib to each other, to achieve higher progress than the other, to make their own richer and more beautiful, to

In the process of globalization, these bases of aesthetic culture change the beauty, cultural progress of the social environment, arising from national and universal values. The person's perception of reality, ideals also enjoy them and express the reality of life in itself. Therefore, in any society, aesthetic culture "is manifested through Real individuals. It consists of a set of individuals whose language, customs, traditions, values have a common spirit of self-realization".

Globalization has created a delicate and complex valeoesthetic education in the development of society, as a result of which the need arose to find a decision on the basis of democratic principles of commonality in the fields of Economics, Education, Science, Culture, Art. As a result, the person's delightful attitude towards Real life events leads to an increase in generality, which pursues vivid spiritual and cultural goals.

In society, these individuals form their valeoesthetic upbringing, which is continuous with aesthetic culture, in the family, relatives, neighborhood, school, etc., developing new concepts in their aesthetic consciousness. On the basis of these, while in the family the father enriches his son with the pride of boyhood, such as courage, valor, honesty, the mother teaches his daughter to be a wise, wise, resourceful, master of beautiful qualities. Relatives, on the other hand, instill more national values, the continuation of the heritage of their ancestors, the members of the neighborhood respect for adults-high aesthetic feelings such as self-esteem for the little ones, inspiration for life if school and striving for an aesthetic culture more in the aesthetic disparity of the child. Today's globalization, in turn, brings in addition to this the achievements of Science and technology in a new way, unique and appropriate, to an environment of Social Beauty.

While Global processes create a wide range of possibilities as a force that positively affects the interests of the Uzbek mentality in the prosperity of society, on the second hand, the individual is bringing into our lives the different images of aesthetic culture, that is, their masks aimed at greater immorality. This thing is mainly "clearly visible in the"non-military spaces" in the way of the Farb culture of globalization, spiritual moral traditions". The subtlety of this issue is the strengthening of the mood of protest against forceful attempts at Farb templates in the world's valeoesthetictarian environment. In this case, Uzbekistan is also calling for the decision of an aesthetic culture corresponding to our national interests, and wide opportunities are being created by our government to develop national values based on democratic principles.

Globalization in an informed society, valeoestheticthe goal is to carry out education through various forms of education in the absorption of education by the individual, in particular, into the minds of young people.

In this case, it is advisable to form the aesthetic culture of a person on the basis of the following tasks on the basis of valeoesthetics:

- the creation of a differential pedagogical-psychological and scientific program of the absorption of valeoesthetics into the consciousness of education in accordance with the age of students and students in all educational institutions;

- continuous monitoring of the formation of aesthetic culture in the absorption of valeoesthetics in the minds of students, based on the national program of training of personnel;

- persistently reflecting the ideas of the national ideology on the basis of aesthetic culture in curricula, textbooks and manuals, inextricably linked with globalization;

- to raise ideological and valeoesthetics in schools, lyceums, colleges, institutes and universities to the level of the requirements of today in a monolithic way to an informed society;

- deepening the knowledge of pedagogical personnel in ideology in each educational institution and deepening the ideas of the information age first of all into their minds and hearts.

Of particular importance is the connection of the aesthetic culture of the individual with the National idea in connection with the media and Centers for the formation of public opinion, as well as the absorption into the consciousness of the younger generation. They are the process of spiritual and educational reforms, the most effective means of quickly reflecting the problems in this regard on various aspects of the life of society. The media, considered the "fourth power", should work on the principles of impartiality and truthfulness, relying on the fact that various opinions open a wide path to colorful views and approaches, awaken a conscious attitude of people to the renewal and changes that occur in our lives.

As a result of the rapid transformation of an informed society, the acceleration of the globalization process and the beginning of the formation of a universal civilization in the 20th century changed the character of World ideologies. The lack of a powerful ideology to replace them, and the change in geopolitical goals further exacerbated the negative effects of these ideas. In such conditions, only a nation that clearly defines its purpose, has a good understanding of needs and interests, has its own beliefs, in a word, has formed its own national idea, retains its future and determines its prospects. The Uzbek people, formed as such a nation, on the basis of their centuries-old national idea, are always ready to enrich the worldview of the individual with progressive texologies, realize identity on the basis of various influences, honor national values and convey aesthetic culture to the future in its own way.

As a result of globalization, the long-standing values that arise from the national mentality of our people were able to make the preservation of aesthetic culture in Ana'ana and traditions their main goal in any conditions.

Binobirin ," any people or nation has its own national, spiritual, natural, cultural characteristics. The Uzbek nation also has a rich spirituality, educational values unique to it. Our people have maintained their true human appearance under any circumstances, the oppression has intensified, the colonial complication, as well as during the periods of their rise. The wonderful rules of morality, spiritual and aesthetic quality and qualities that underlie the upbringing of a harmonious generation have been instilled from generation to generation over the centuries." It was the supreme manifestation of aesthetic culture, which was harmonized with high human qualities and feelings.

Seeing these qualities that make up the valeoesthetic education of our people as the main goal of social life, its effective use in the homogenization and globalization of today's world, serves to find a solution to the pressing problem. We strive to create a pleasure relationship, always vigilantly from the various pressures and ideological struggles that exist in society, to give rise to the necessary conditions for our education to live alert to the forces that impose their mask, especially the high aesthetic culture and spirituality that leads to a bright future. At the moment, the process of globalization in our country, its influence on the National idea, is also a common law. This process increases their interdependence, interaction in the lives of different countries, peoples, does not remain without reflection in their spiritual, ideological life. But in what way and to what extent it is used is a sign of the internal problem and social progress of each state. We all see aspects of different cultures and values floating in different information streams that have a strong influence on the individual in processes in the social environment, in particular in activities with aesthetic cultures disguised in relation to the human mind and soul.

More such cases are manifested in the fact that " at the present stage of globalization of the information space, the relationship of the internet with national and international campaigns, the Periodical Press, TV and radio is expanding even more. Hence, the further liberalization of media activities is the demand of the period. The harmonization of the press of Uzbekistan with the world media system, the integration of the Internet into the global information space are clearly visible." It is a matter of concern that we use these effective components that serve for the individual, providing wide opportunities for his perspective and future, encouraging the release of the aesthetic culture of society into higher paganism.

Today, the media are gaining a positive

character for the development of the aesthetic culture of the individual in society on the one hand, forming in the consciousness and thinking, culture of people, giving beauty to the social environment, ensuring their convergence, on the other hand, as a result of the abundance of information, a person creates wide opportunities to compare which country or, thirdly, in the aesthetic ideas of this information aimed at the formation of pleasure relationships, masked cultures, which are sometimes sad for the fate of the nation and Man, serve to poison the minds of the younger generation more[61].

The richness of the aesthetic culture of the individual is directly buried in the ocean of enormous information, which should be understandable to those who are dealing with this knowledge in order to ensure the success of one or another activity of a person. Otherwise, it is also possible that people who use it themselves knowingly threaten the development of society, valeoesthetic education.

Ensuring that globalization in the field of information is aimed at protecting an individual's interests is an urgent problem of our society. But

---

[61] Göyibnazarov Sh. Popular culture. - T.: Uzbekistan, 2012. P. 166.

it should be embodied in each of our activities to comprehensively master the processes affecting the worldview and spiritual education of the individual, to look for mechanisms for the effective functioning of factors in the development of aesthetic culture, to introduce into society the age-old values and mentality that can fight against the destructive views of various ideas and ideologies. In our society, the presence of certain common ideas, values that develop the aesthetic culture of the individual "has always regulated the interaction of people. A national idea based on universal values also plays a unifying role for a multiethnic country[62]".

The fact that globalization opens up wide opportunities for media activities has a huge impact on valeoesthetic education, which serves as an important factor in the development of the aesthetic culture of the individual in Uzbekistan. This upbringing also contributes to the development of national values, traditions and traditions of our people, religious rituals and udums.

In the context of today's globalization, the

---

[62] Ergashev I., Sharipov B., Jakbarov M. Liberalization of society and spirituality. - T.: Academia, 2002. P. 26.

possibilities of information in the present have intensified. To do this, it is not necessary to destroy a nation-a nation, a people-as a nation, by pouring a bomb on its head and losing it. It is only enough to keep this people away from their values. Indeed, within all the available means and weapons in the world, the information medium is now becoming even more terrible than any significant military weapon. Any bomb kills or physically weakens a limited number of people at once. The information bomb, on the other hand, makes millions and millions of people, especially young people, morally-mentally ill and crippled every day. They are made alive mistresses, who have renounced their parents, homeland and national values, are capable of any inhumane affairs, do not know God either or are given to religious mutuality, while Pride, violence and Abyss have become their usual qualities.

Of the current types and manifestations of information – the so-called "mass culture" - is the most naughty. The most dangerous thing about"mass culture" is that in it, the laws of beauty, experiences and skills that make Lies True, inclinations inherent in almost all people, various legendary historical events, the possibilities of the psyche, art, philosophy, religion, politics, and so on, skillfully using them, the most subtle aspects of youth are influenced, their sexual, national and other emotions are carved, they are brought to

"Today, however, the forces of the Eastern family that set themselves the goal of undermining traditional rules are found. Although they do not act with cruelty and ignorance, like the previous tyrants, from this the essence of their behavior does not change. It turns out even, on the contrary. Such benefactors are trying to instill in the current youth of Central Asia a fiction about a "new right family" using the tested method of "using soft force". Currently, the consciousness of the youth of our country is clogged by the system of technologies and pirncips of Western society, which caused negative consequences in European countries, through the powerful mechanism of influence of mass culture .

We must constantly avoid these situations that are intensely entering the information space, create conditions for the development of aesthetic cultures that serve to elevate valeoesthetic education in society.

It is also historically known that the spiritual values practiced in society are founded on the loss of its future if it is trampled upon. This situation arose more with a negative orientation of the criteria of morality, which is a form of important social consciousness in society. Such a situation " trampling on the spiritual value of non-adultery, which was deified by the Christian religion in a number of European countries in the Middle Ages, caused the urgency of pride, perversion and immorality in society. In particular, the vices of immorality at the court of the French kings or Catherine II are known from history. It is remarkable that some works written during this period praised the seduction of one's wife, adultery, as heroic rather than sinful" .

Today's Western world, which is turning the immorality and prostitution that developed in the Middle Ages into their own head idea, seeks to subjugate the ideological-spiritual upbringing of an individual. They chose such a path as a spiritual weapon of world domination.

These vices, which threaten human culture and morality, are at the same time trying to reject aesthetic cultures that praise goodness and beauty. Such deep-rooted ideological-spiritual upbringing in the Farb world rightly interprets neither religion nor secularism. They are terribly clinging to all regions of the earth without choosing nationality and religion, striving to scatter the seeds of spiritual disgrace. On the basis of these false concepts, the interests of the people, any positive traits and character that serve for the future of mankind, we will not find. At the same time," it is especially alarming that the moral abyss, which gnaws at Man as a divine being, loses its roots, grows into a powerful and cruel propaganda weapon in the hands of someone, firmly occupying modern media – Internet networks, in the art of cinema and variety, in fiction, in the media."

The wide penetration of globalization into the information world is trying to instill a lot of unnecessary information in the aesthetic culture and ideological and spiritual education of the individual. Billions of information, which spread to the world through the media every day, show their new image and meaning. As a result, there is an increasing desire among young people to acquire more modern information, and as a result, the dangers that threaten the future of the nation are entering our lives more widely.

In order to preserve ideological and spiritual education in our society from such foreign ideas and worldviews, we must make our national mentality strong and our faith strong. Because the fact that our people have a special high aesthetic culture is a sign that they preserve our rich cultural assets and historical heritage as if they were eyebrows. It is lozarb in life to honor our glorious values, which have been revered for centuries, to strive to raise our honor and pride higher.

Traditions that develop the worldview of our people in their original way serve as a component of folk spirituality, an important moral value, a means of upbringing. Folk traditions, etiquette manifested in the process of rituals, kindness, honor, qualities such as Honor are important in the formation of youth spirituality. This, in turn, is evidence that our country has put spirituality and spiritual education on the agenda as an urgent problem from the earliest days of independence, providing wide opportunities for special attention and care to young people.

The head of our far-sighted state began his life in the new century on the basis of a policy aimed at elevating the aesthetic culture of the individual. Focusing on ideological and spiritual education in society, he began to take all measures to be aware of the immoralities and culturalities that began to occur in the developed countries of the world in the 20th century, not to let them enter our lives. This was our great history and aesthetic culture, which BI inherited from our ancestors. However, Mukhammadzhan Quronov wrote that " as early as the 80s of the last century, strange clubs of spouses began to appear in the United States. These clubs hosted various bazmi jamshids, shows, entertainment nights. Usually they were made by a couple and came together. At the height of the occupation, the couple was given to another man, and the wife "used"her husband to another woman. When the passions were suppressed and the souls were bleeding, the couple returned home again, as if they had seen nothing, gladly" .

The threat of Farb culture to the development of society also directly leads to a violation of ideological and spiritual education. This is reported by Professor Timothy J. at the University of Cambridge.In uniter's "Islam in the 21st century", he writes: "of the 900 priests who preach in the context of London's family values,

200 tend towards homosexuality, homophily (male-to-male sexuality). In Britain, 34% of children are born without marriage, with so many adults suffering from the pain of divorce".

The bottomless and disgusting work of those who are immersed in such a vile swamp cannot be an example of aesthetic culture for any individual. It is darcor that we become aware of them and develop our valeoesthetics, referring repeatedly to our past, to our national values. National value is a sign of high respect for the people's past, today and future, the development of Science and culture, national morality. Therefore, in the current period, it is important to pay special attention to national values in the performance of urgent tasks in the field of Education.

The harmonization of globalization with education will be directly related to the psyche and spiritual world of the individual. The formation of aesthetic culture and upbringing in young people should be combined with the ideas of the homeland in which he was born and raised. The child can be taught Exact Sciences, work on modern computers, in foreign countries or with the help of representatives of these countries, but there is no need to prove that love for the motherland, the familiar and veneration of the motherland, the feeling of always present for its protection, should be formed only and only in this country, Because for a person, first of all, spiritual education begins with the ground on which the blood of the navel is drained. Enjoying it, he forms his spirituality, aesthetic culture. Therefore, we must instill our valeoesthetics in the minds of our children, and young people, through each old husband of our motherland. Negative aesthetic cultures, like the one above, which otherwise threaten the future, are embedded in the consciousness and thinking of our people, while chaos of different manifestations causes atrocities towards science.

An important feature of globalization in a time when the ideological landscape of the world is becoming diverse is the expansion of the possibilities of an ideological-spiritual sphere of influence for an individual and, as a result, the transformation of aesthetic culture in all regions of the Earth into a universal problem. In this situation, each country will have to have a national mentality that can maintain its identity, protect against the influence of harmful ideas and cultures. In our country, the well-being of the people and the prospect of the country are aimed at transforming such ideological and spiritual education into the faith and faith of the individual, bringing to adulthood the perfect people in society.

The prosperity of each state or society and the enjoyment of people will depend on the behavior, moral ideals, aesthetic culture and spiritual maturity of the children of this country. This is reflected in the view of the enlightened jadidist Abdullah Avlani that "discipline is for us either a matter of life, or of salvation, or of destruction, or of bliss, or of disaster".

The organization of ideological and spiritual education of people on the basis of these words ensures that high feelings about life, a pleasure attitude towards reality are perfect. The desire, competence and skills for beauty and art in men elevate the position of artistic-aesthetic and ideological-spiritual education in society.

Based on valeoesthetic upbringing, it is relevant that every parent, teacher, teacher teach the younger generation that the correct perception of beauty in life and art, the upbringing and upbringing of aesthetic needs in a person, globalization is a factor that provokes delicate aesthetic cultures.

In providing valeoesthetic education to our children, from an early age, it is necessary to enrich the worldview with a world of sophistication, instilling in the mind the tone of music, the freshness and beauty of elegant flowers, the cultivation of works of art, the beauty of the objective universe, being able to distinguish its diverse manifestations. Especially in the ideological and spiritual education of students at school classes of literature, music, painting, etc. In such an upbringing, the desire for an aesthetic culture in the spiritual and material life of society goes to kuchaya.

An important feature of globalization in the process of valeoesthetic education is that it is of great importance in educating individuals in mental, moral, physical terms of their mutual pleasure attitude towards each other. Observing reality, ideological-spiritual upbringing in satisfying various needs in society gives a person spiritual strength.

The person always dreams that his marriage is sweet, his life is spent with landscapes rich in goodness and beauty. On this basis, from the very beginning of the formation of the personality society, the individual sought to enrich valeoesthetic, to harmonize the meaning and content of the essence of the world of elegance with aesthetic culture. As a result, the individual, with his practical and aesthetic activity, tried to assimilate reality and change it, to create a "second nature"that would delight a person. Beauty and ugliness in reality, distinguish laughter and tragedy from each other, realizing what the true essence of the world is. These are all made possible by the requirements and needs of the individual for their survival. Here are such feelings, experiences that develop an aesthetic culture in the process of valeoesthetic education. However, if a human child lives among animals, then no upbringing will decide. Perhaps animals live life in accordance with their lifestyle. Such cases we read through many works of art and watched in motion pictures. Society is so complex and interesting that a person can also educate an animal. But the ideological-spiritual upbringing of the animal does not serve for the development of aesthetic culture.

Speaking about globalization, aesthetic factors should also be taken into account. On this basis, it is advisable to realize certain aesthetic qualities in the absorption of valeoesthetic education into the consciousness of the individual and, on this basis, to carry out the process of upbringing. Therefore, valeoesthetictarbia never requires a certain amount of time from a person. Maybe every step we take will continue to be our companion in our lives with different characteristics and encourage us to be highly aesthetically cultured, responsible, resilient, resilient.

Aesthetic culture, based on the past in the process of valeoesthetic upbringing, enriches the present into an invaluable unique beauty. The individual develops cultural and aesthetic education by delivering his aesthetic culture to the future on the basis of succession, attributing the valeoesthetic upbringing in them to the beauty of the past. The strengthening of interest in the world of sophistication in man, the formation of culture and spirituality, which reflect their own shine in values, is of great importance in the development of a new society as the basis of valeoesthetic upbringing in the context of globalization. Aesthetic culture and spirituality in each person is manifested, first in his valeoesthetic upbringing in the family, and then in the aesthetic perception of the beauty of the whole world under the influence of social associations. There is an aesthetic culture and national spirituality of all nations and elates in the world, which is important in the valeoesthetic education of the younger generation, studied in depth by future generations.

Since the valeoesthetic upbringing of a person is manifested in its aesthetic culture and national spirituality, it should always embody such feelings as feeling beauty on the basis of these, enjoying the beauty of the world of elegance, having good qualities and qualities. Therefore, the aesthetic upbringing of an individual is perfect, and the appearance of Sergio is directly related to spiritual-cultural aspects. Through these, the individual develops not only a sense of beauty, but also an aesthetic culture based on his high feelings, habits, skills and qualifications. In particular, in order for aesthetic culture and national spirituality to correspond to the bright stars, ideology of its time and the demands and needs of the era, valeoestetiktarbia must be strong. Because, in any valeoestetiktarbiya, there must be harmony, unity, proportionality of aesthetic culture and national spirituality. If the temple does not exist such qualities, then spiritual perfection and aesthetic needs cannot meet the demand of the Times.

In the context of today's globalization, our aesthetic culture and spirituality, in which the spirit of nationalism is instilled in the realization of such aspects in the process of aesthetic education, is aimed at quickly and vigilantly feeling the beauty in life from us, burking our entire spiritual world, social relations in the world of sophistication. In particular, the joy of the day-to-day beauty of our cities and villages, as well as the beautiful and beautiful beauty of our pleasure-rich khushmanzara Mother Nature, will delight the soul of a person. Full breathing from such feelings brings into the aesthetic culture and spiritual world of the individual the passions of latophobia and femininity.

How majestic the process of globalization in society is to aesthetic ideas based on nationality, and rich in sharp and subtle feelings that a person can find a place in his heart at once, means that there is a long history of our aesthetic culture and spirituality, filled with a deep past, joy and joy. The individual continues to increase his aesthetic needs through his valeoesthetic upbringing, and to cup values that enrich his aesthetic culture. The organization of the harmony of valeoesthetics and aesthetic culture embodies the feelings of high sophistication in the individual. To the aesthetic ideals of human life, it turns monotheism, aesthetic exegesis into an interesting and murakab aesthetic Dargah. At the moment, the areas of aesthetic culture and spirituality that affect the true beauty of life are represented in literature and art by beautiful and elegant artistic images. This increases the artistic power of aesthetic forgiveness and needs, leading the individual towards beauty with high feelings of aesthetic culture and spiritual perfection. Independence in Uzbekistan is carried out on the basis of the national values of valeoestetiktarbia, which is carried out in the years. Because on the basis of national values, aesthetic culture and national spirituality have hidden their invaluable masterpiece. The absorption of this masterpiece into the minds of the cherished younger generation, the application of the unique ideological and spiritual education, inherited from centuries to centuries, to social life in the era of globalization, is valuable for our aesthetic culture as an eyeshadow of a perfect and attractive feeling. The ideological and spiritual education of our people created the civilization of Central Asia, which embodied a period of more than three thousand years. Our valeoesthetic upbringing is characterized by the aesthetic aspects inherent in this civilization: the realization of the beauty of the place of birth and the motherland, the richness of the world of generational elegance with new aesthetic visions, always respect for adults, enjoyment in circulation, aesthetic culture and serjilo swings of national spirituality. All this is a feeling of pride, which demonstrates the exalted beauty of the valeoesthetic upbringing of our descendants-ancestors, the contribution of their spiritual heritage to the entire world civilization, the height of dignity, prestige.

With its aesthetic education, our people realize not only national pride, aesthetic culture and national spirituality, but also the beauty of nature as the totality of society, the non-progressive aspects of human artistic thinking. Every person who loves his nationality is proud, enjoys the world of people's achievements, prestige, beauty, with his spiritual feelings, inner experiences, seeks to add beauty to his beauty. A person of high national pride, ideological and spiritual upbringing venerates the aesthetic culture of his soul, appreciates his national spirituality with rare works and the heritage of a colorful illuminator, rejoices in the fact that he has a great past. The fact that a person enriches his valeoesthetic upbringing forms a high feeling of mastering his material, spiritual heritage, perfect knowledge of customs, traditions, values.

Globalization in all areas, with valeoesthetic upbringing, the aesthetic culture is inextricably reflecting the exciting, passionate manifestations of our social life. In particular, it is advisable to develop national spirituality, to develop a national language and aesthetic culture, to study national self-awareness, national feelings, national pride and aesthetic education in harmony with each other in their wonderful manifestations. The development of an independent Uzbekistan has changed the culture of thinking, working, lifestyle of members of society in a new way based on the laws of elegance. It is gratifying that a similar worldview is being formed in the youth valeoesthetictarbia. The essence of aesthetic culture, which has formed a whole chain of it to the present day, should be brought into the hearts of people, starting from the foundations of the upbringing of elegance, in order to fully show the all-powerful, deep and colorful nature of the educational foundations of our spirituality, its deep and colorful existence, its But, at the same time, the effect of what is being done, the place of ideological and spiritual education in society cannot be called complete and perfect. In the world of human life, lifestyle, spiritual, aesthetic culture and national spirituality are not without some shortcomings. To do this, only then will the goals that we set ourselves bear fruit if the whole nation organizes the knowledge that it gives in maturing its younger generation, initially in connection with aesthetic culture.

Valeoesthetictarbia, in the context of globalization, always has its influence on social relationships with its color and variety. A person's feeling of beauty in reality, as a result of his aesthetic activity, gives pleasure to himself with his work. This, in turn, raises the role of aesthetic culture in our society to the point of achieving all-round maturity.

As a result of globalization, various contradictions in social life, the decision-making of a prosperous life in society causes the emergence in a person of a social, political, spiritual, moral, aesthetic, cultural spiritual environment that is important for aesthetic culture. Here, on the basis of these, aesthetic culture becomes associated with valeoestetiktarbiya. the property of bias arises. This is an important factor in the development of the social background, economic, legal, scientific, ideological views of each society.

In Uzbekistan, which manifests itself day after day in the world, today valeoesthetics, a characteristic feature of Austria, is enriched with a world of elegance.

First of all, thanks to independence, all conditions are created for the free functioning of the individual, and people objectively approach reality on the basis of their aesthetic taste, independent thinking, aspiration, creative ability. In them, globalization forms concepts and visions that are carriers of positive emotions leading to the formation of an aesthetic culture that serves society, the people.

Secondly, globalization connects the people with a way of life, the succession of aesthetic ideals between the past and the present, manifesting the versatility of our aesthetic consciousness by influencing the development of valeoesthetic education and culture of citizens by the achievements of science.

Thirdly, in the construction of the legal democratic civil society, it is manifested that the production and market relations are improved, life is complicated, and the spirituality, culture and valeoesthetic education of citizens are connected by national and modern traditions.

Fourth, the 21st century, the age of technology, shows that not all sciences can develop without globalization. As a result, the organization of production on the basis of the achievements of the latest science should develop its aesthetic activity in life, strengthening people's confidence in the future. In humans, there is an increase in the development of aesthetic culture, ensuring loyalty to their profession, spiritual values.

Fifth, it is necessary to convey to people how the system of "fourth power", which adorns our daily life and gives us new knowledge of the universe, has an impact on valeoesthetic education. On this basis, it is necessary to form aesthetic ideals, feelings, high spirituality.

Sixth, due to the demand of the period, it is darcor to widely introduce the "National Program of Personnel Training" into society. In the process of valeoesthetic education of young people, strong contact with foreign countries and constant awareness of the news that is happening in the world in the field of education is one of the urgent tasks.

2.3§. Factors and prospects for raising aesthetic culture in the Uzbek mentality

The 21st century, together with the beginning of a new historical era for Humanity, also gave rise to a process of comprehensive globalization and integralization. These circumstances, which shaped its lush appearance on every aspect of society, led to the development of bleaching and synergistic approaches to modern values. As a result of this, even in the field of national mentality, aspirations, visions, aesthetic ideals, moral norms for the acquisition of human consciousness and soul began to take their toll on social life. The reflection of modernity in each individual, in which a delightful attitude towards the assimilation of national-artistic values, gives a new worldview and a spiritual world. Modern aesthetic culture "the social need is growing for individuals who have realized national values in the current international context, where the process of globalization is going on around the world, and the ideological struggle for the minds and hearts of people is at its peak, who are able to protect it. It is a necessity to bring up competent people who can fully meet the requirements of this new historical situation, being seen as a natural and legitimate situation." Because in every activity that penetrates deeply into the life of an individual from an aesthetic point of view, factors such as feelings of high humanity, sharp didiness are becoming the demands and needs of today. [63]

As a result of the conditions of independence and globalization, the free maturation of each individual is finding an aesthetic culture that is important to provide the necessary opportunities for everyone to live in society with pleasure relationships.

The process of globalization, combined with the transformation of the spiritual image of our people, leads to the modernization of the aesthetic culture of the individual, that is, to a gradual renewal of his spiritual and emotional feelings. As a result, the elegance in the use of aesthetic education and culture of society is becoming more relevant day by day. Because we must carry out our spirituality, national values, moral criteria, customs, traditions and rituals, which are taking shape on the basis of aesthetic

---

[63] Karimov Ibrokhim. Honor of the nation. - T.: New century generation, 2005. P. 16.

culture, safely taking away from the various struggles that are taking place in the information field. Also, the importance and relevance of this issue is growing even more, given the rapid spread of events and actions taking place all over the world, namely, in the present moment, when the process of globalization is taking place in the world, including in the world of Informatics. In order to correctly establish the expected results, we must first of all develop a national upbringing and aesthetic activity aimed at ensuring that our aesthetic culture is kept up with the Times.

The fact that we conduct our aesthetic culture in society on the basis of thorough plans and programs aimed at the intended goals demonstrates that our spirituality is broader in scope, more practical in importance. Therefore, each of us is required by our time to educate the future generation of aesthetic tastes and high spirituality on the basis of our past heritage. In the process of globalization, "the world today is discovering Uzbekistan through its national-cultural heritage, rich history, language, culture, embodiment of Customs and traditions with universal ideas, achievements in the field of art and architecture, science and culture. So we can also become active promoters, not just passive receivers in the process of globalization". Only then can we manifest ourselves as the original successors and developing entities of modern aesthetic culture and values.

The national-artistic values that the Uzbek people have formed and developed over the centuries have, to this day, widely covered all spheres of our social life. The development of national-artistic values in the Uzbek family is characterized by its sides, which are not directly similar to other folk families in the world. Because the role of the family in providing aesthetic education and the formation of aesthetic taste for Uzbek children is incomparable. The first goal in teaching aesthetic culture to the child of today should be the good-natured, courteous words of the parents, the correct understanding of beautiful, showy reality, the comprehensive knowledge that they give to the younger generation, be clear and bright, not based on old-fashioned views and things left behind in our time.

In each Uzbek household, the upbringing of aesthetic culture in a national spirit, the formation of aesthetic feelings in them and the maturation of elegant feelings is the main task in the prospect. Of great importance in the formation of aesthetic culture in the family is the pleasure attitude towards tevarak-surroundings (neighborhood, neighborhood, kindergarten, school, etc.), observation of the beauty of reality, perception and education of aesthetic sense, taste, ideal. It is also necessary to educate them by instilling an admiration for the beauty and art of nature, but to develop an aesthetic culture based on modern national-artistic values, and not art masked by global processes.

In the process of globalization, in addition to the universal concept of beauty inherent in other peoples in the Uzbek people, there is an aesthetic culture unique only to this people. There are many different opinions on this identity in many countries around the world. It can be seen from this that the Uzbek family seeks to create its own future, based on its past. In particular, there is a growing comparison of older family members with the height of their aesthetic culture, strong interests in fiction and art, their aesthetic pleasure directly affecting young children in global processes, with social life. From an early age, the child has a deeper understanding of the difference between good and bad, beautiful and ugly concepts when his aesthetic culture is perfect. In the absorption of such concepts into the consciousness of a young child, first of all, one should take into account their interests. If parents notice that the child has an interest in something, sports or a certain area of art, it is useful for him to attract them to these interests.

In some cases, parents are attracted to homesick homes without considering the interests of their children. Also, some parents are busy with their work and do not pay good attention to the upbringing of a child, his behavior and aesthetic culture.

A child raised in this state will find it difficult to find his place in society. For this reason, each parent must respond to society for the upbringing and aesthetic world of their child. To our social life "the migration of foreign films and publications in a public way, the prevalence of audio and video tapes, faith and national identity have not yet been fully formed, or the level is impacting people with poor mentality. The habit of dressing and treating, the national moral criteria, the blurring of nationalism in musical culture, the restriction from classical music and literature, grandfathers ' oaths and signs, book reading, of course, cannot have a negative impact on the value of national values." Therefore, it is advisable for each of us to mature aesthetic culture on the basis of our national and artistic values in the family, without associating it with European life, which is measured only by Joy and exuberance, comfort.

Such situations are characterized simply by the insistence in the Uzbek family that the parents have affection, sweet words associated with the culture of treatment, to honor what they like, to be passionate about what they do. On the basis of such an aesthetic culture, conversation, free communication form aesthetic feelings and sharp didlity. In the formation of our modern national and artistic values, aesthetic culture begins with a cheerful attitude towards life in each individual, focusing on observing the beauty of reality in the aesthetic spirit, feeling the beauty of the surroundings, cultivating a high sense of nature.

Conditions are of great importance as an important factor in the absorption of modern nationalism into the younger generation. If the house in which the child lives is saramjom-competent and tidy, it will be the order in the

House. In the house where the child lives, there is always order, saramjomlik, ozadalik, the child, starting at a young age, forms good habits, skills in himself. He is used to being tidy, dressing with taste, tidying up his bed space and training weapons. So, our national-artistic values connect themselves with aesthetic culture, starting with the bosom of the family.

Even in any globalization, our people are developing their own aesthetic culture, not forgetting about their national values. Today, do not go to any corner of our country, clean yards like porcelain, houses sorted by taste, beautiful streets are very-very much. Our people love to make the yard clean and cool and cozy, sprinkling all over the summer. Such wonderful habits and qualities are taught to more young girls and brides in the Uzbek family. They wake up prematurely every day, and the children sort out a lot of things until they get up. All this is the fact that the long-standing aesthetic culture of our people is preserved and manifests itself in a way that suits our times.

In the Uzbek family, each child is brought up in the way of being with a delicate taste, being able to appreciate the beauty of reality, understanding artistic culture. In the upbringing of a child, his intelligence, aesthetic sense, attitude to fiction and art, desires are important. Therefore, parents sought to make their children understand, feel the beauty and ugliness of marriage, to master the spiritual qualities of people. Their children developed in their hearts such moods as hard work, sweet eloquence, joy, warmth, smile, and in any modernity taught to be faithful to the national-artistic values of our ancestors.

Through such a culture, parents explained to their children the beauty of the soul, the spiritual maturation of the individual. Even the past manifested our spirituality in their minds. Therefore, even in any globalization and modernity, our wise people did not say in vain "beautiful husnu is not in Jamal, but in fazlu Kamal"!

One of the important factors of national upbringing as a high aesthetic value in the Uzbek family is the firmness of the father and maternal kindness. For the father invites his child from a young age to be fond of work, to be proud of the beauty of reality, to walk, to be highly aesthetically gifted in art, and to walk away from disgusting and ugly, tasteless events. In the heart of her child, high human feelings, inner and outer beauty strive to mature mental sharpness. And the mother, in addition to these more, tries to equalize her child with pleasant singing, music, walk in the bosom of beautiful nature, watch beautiful landscapes and fill her heart with joy, etc.

The role of our older grandparents in the development of national and artistic values in the Uzbek family and the upbringing of the younger generation in an aesthetic spirit is also incomparably greater. They fall in love with and caress their grandchildren, giving them their overflowing love in their hearts. They tell their grandchildren about the joys and worries of life. Often speaking fairy tales, narratives and stories, he urges them to be Dipper, brave, fearless humble, pure, beautiful, beautiful. In particular, the beauty of nature, telling each of its creatures one by one of its extraordinary qualities, makes a decision in the children's worldview of subtle emotions, aesthetic ideals and aesthetic culture.

The aesthetic culture of the Uzbek people, inherited from centuries to centuries, in the process of globalization, it is also advisable to use the culture, unique masterpieces of our people and the humor of ilmu wisdom in educating young people, creating a latent, feminine, Lobar excellent mood in their minds. Therefore, every child raised today in an Uzbek family should first of all grow up full of pleasure from our past heritage and values, and, moreover, grow up full of the aesthetic culture of the peoples of the world, turning a bright future Uzbekistan into a beautiful land of high feelings.

In any context, a person is considered an excellent trait behavior that manifests its aesthetic culture. Each person is associated with a walk, an oshno heart to beauty, noble and compassionate feelings, sincere expressions of heart, upbringing in the behavior of true beauty. All sorts of Proverbs used among our people are manifested, first of all, in the family in the harmony, pure love, sophistication, loyalty of parents to each other. The high aesthetic culture inherited from the past is revered as a national value even in our time. Therefore, a well-mannered, heavy-handed, wise mother keeps assigning her married daughter every time she sees her, "respect my son-in-law". It is necessary to realize how well-mannered beautiful feelings and age-old examples of aesthetic culture are reflected in these words

Zamiri. How much a couple respects each other in the family, behavior is manifested directly before the eyes of their children. In the family, parental restraint, behavior, habit are clearly reflected in their aesthetic and moral upbringing.

Among our people, it can be seen that modern national-artistic values are simply deeply reflected in family relationships. In any modernity, both husband and wife, that is, the parent, must have the same pleasure in both the joy and anxiety of the family, in their fasting, and in the educational process of their children. Based on national-artistic values, the cohabitation of the couple is of great importance in family rocking, raising children and introducing Grace into the House. In particular, the agility of a housewife, her Beautiful, Tidy and orderly disposition of the house, her constant dressing of her children with taste, her presence in a pazan eliminates any spiritual and physical drawback.

Among our people, modern national-artistic values are more associated with women. The fact that women prepare a delicious dish, are cheeky in sewing clothes, Achilles and shirinso add husn to their Husn and bring joy, beauty, fairies into the family. Our people are hospitable and seek to cheerfully welcome the guest, who, under any circumstances, stumbled upon the door to his house. Even the petty gins, which sometimes remain in the family, quickly disappear with the arrival of the guest. Here in such cases, aesthetic culture comes first. It is necessary that we young people also get to know this thing well. Because, this stream of life leads every person over time to such a khushmanzara family. Therefore, the fact that every young man-girl, during his life, embodies the beautiful qualities of his parents ' marriage, learns from an early age the aesthetic culture of the family, rich in mystery-synoat, is a reminder that in the future he will grow up to become a wonderful family owner and hostess.

We can also see the factors of globalization that sometimes negatively affect individual spirituality and aesthetic culture. This thing often manifests itself on the street, on holidays, at weddings, at meetings. After all, everywhere a person needs to dress neatly, clean his soul, pay attention to beauty in his walk. Because without taste, in addition to lagging behind in our time, a person with a crumpled head and head that reflect primitiveness in himself, without a beard, with barked hair, looks cold to the eye. Compactness and ugliness make a person even more beautiful when he walks, paying attention to his appearance. But modernity in some girls and women is due to over-growing nails, shaving short hair, over-grooming, getting dressed strangely, especially in the summer months, revealing the navel and shoulder, wearing earrings on the navel and nose, hanging rows of beads around the neck, wearing two to three large-large earrings on the ears, looks ugly. But a person with a real aesthetic culture manifests himself in behavior with a beautiful walk, beautiful posture, beautiful speaking.

There are also national-artistic values \ u200b \ u200bof our people, which are not perceived from the outside, and there are also factors in the form of certain laws and regulations, moral criteria. First, in the early morning, the Reaper is pulled up and the gate or door of the house is opened. Because, among the people, there is a saying that" food is shared at dawn." Also, the morning air will be clear, the sound of the bird's wanderings will give a feeling of peace to the soul of a person. Secondly, the situation is not asked without washing the face-hand, after washing the face-hand, the little ones greet the adults. Women prepare breakfast, girls, brides sweep the yard, street door and sprinkle with water. These high national values serve today to develop an aesthetic culture that brings grace and blessing to our cities and villages.

The globalization process requires the person to approach reality with a delightful attitude, to form an aesthetic culture that gives a natural latency and sophistication to a person's behavior. In the implementation of such a culture, it is useful for the future that adults, without sparing their precious time, pay attention to the fact that young sprouts will grow up ugly and beautiful. Because, by nature, the child is imitative and can immediately advance what he sees, the word he hears. Such imitation in a child greatly affects his aesthetic culture, causing his behavior to be rich in a sense of beauty and vital aesthetic ideals. Because the behavior, treatment, taste, intelligence, gait, dress, mind and perception of older people, housekeeping are not overlooked by the child. Older people may not pay attention to this, but the child always looks at Zim. However, imitation is a child's means of studying human qualities, aesthetic experiences. Therefore, childhood in the House should not allow older people to commit indecent behavior and rude acts, to set an example for children in all respects, that is, morality, decency and aesthetics. That is why it is bad for a child to say obscene words in front of him, to make a pretense, to make mistakes, to raise a child. Through the upbringing of elegance, it is taught to follow the long-standing Oriental custom, rules of etiquette in the process of cooking, sitting around the table and eating. It is on the basis of such an aesthetic culture that children in the family pay more attention to the beauty of family relationships. It is also not for nothing that the folk proverb says that he "does what he sees in the bird's nest". On the basis of this proverb, a deep life truth, spirituality and culture can be seen dripping. From this point of view, in the emergence of a child's high aesthetic culture, personal feelings and moral qualities, the omnipresent presence of large people in the family is associated with aesthetic culture.

The upbringing of children in the family is influenced by the attitude of family members to each other, the behavior of parents, neighbors and other relatives, culture of treatment, aesthetic ideals. If the family members are tidy, tidy, well-behaved, the more beautiful feelings the child's upbringing will be.

Since the family is the first place for the formation of aesthetic culture, the role of radio and television is incomparably greater in making the child have a perfect and mature aesthetic feeling in all respects. Especially many TV series and simply cartoons that are shown on television are also passing a means of negative impact on the minds of our children.

As young people, children like to listen to fairy tales, stories on the radio, and on television to see interesting multflms. All this is the main factor in the formation of aesthetic culture in the growth of children's consciousness, the colorization of their worldview. Especially now, the influence of television on the upbringing of children is strong. In perspective, children should only be limited to showing them self-sufficient shows. Sitting a child in front of the TV for hours can not only affect his health, but also cause him to begin to verbally perceive a work of art. In the upbringing of a child, this process sharpens thinking, matures new ideas of knowledge and sophistication. Therefore, it is advisable for every family to be attracted to listening to the radio or watching TV, taking into account the interests of children. But in most apartments, mostly adults ignore the interest of the child and see a broadcast or show with their own disillusionment. This may not correspond to the worldview of a young child. The child also sits in the parental row and watches all kinds of horror movies, and he himself comes to look like the heroes in these movies. As a result, various changes occur in the child's consciousness, and spiritually his consciousness becomes poisoned. This, in turn, can lead to various negative consequences. Therefore, when all children in the family are listened to the broadcasts that they need from an early age in accordance with their worldview, and children are watched with age-appropriate gestures, the life of the family will be beautiful and prosperous the next day.

Each day, turning into the past, with its traditions remains sealed in the memory of the future generation. Traditions are national-artistic values of material and spiritual forms of activity, communication and relations between people, which are manifested in various spheres of life of society, inherited from generation to generation. Historically it is known that there is no people who do not have any of their own traditions and traditions, national values. All peoples, demonstrating their identity on the basis of their traditions, tried to shape their children's aesthetic culture. Any nation or people has always preserved their traditions and carried out their lifestyle, spiritual maturation in a way that depends on aesthetic education. It is always characterized by the fact that the traditions of one era change over time, increasing or decreasing in aesthetic significance in a second period, and the emergence of others. For this reason, it happens that the traditions and aesthetic thinking of one period do not correspond to the second period or are forgotten.

Due to Uzbekistan's independence, increasing globalization, the emphasis on our national-artistic values and traditions has increased. In our national values, there is a peculiarity in beautiful traditions, paintings, rituals and traditions that are not like other peoples of the world. As you know, values are formed under certain conditions. For this reason, they are manifested in local, regional, national content and Universal appearance. The most aesthetically and morally mature of local values and suitable for national interests are gradually sorted out and raised to a nationwide level. And in the National Environment, aesthetic culture is decided on the basis of traditions. Understanding and reacting to traditions through aesthetic culture shifts the focus of respect for one's own nation, Eli, land, and the aesthetic culture of other nations. Therefore, the increase in the aesthetic culture of the people serves greatly, first of all, to increase interest in our traditions, as well as the role of aesthetic education in society.

We can also see the traditions of the Uzbek people in the process of globalization today, when the great allomas al-Khwarizmi, Farabi, Beruniy, Ibn Sina, who were able to pluck the flowers of the highest peaks of World Science in several languages, spied on the world in their works. They perfectly knew not only the traditions of their people, their painting, and, moreover, the traditions of other peoples. In particular, Abu Rayhon Beruniy went to India to write his work" India", where he studied the Hindi language, customs, rituals, traditions, culture, beautiful nature, the khushmanzara mountains perfectly. On this basis he created"India".

In the context of globalization, national-artistic values and traditions are one of the ways to develop an aesthetic culture of the individual, to teach him the experiences of the older generation. Many of our traditions, which are aimed at losing during the time of the saloars in the moment, are being revived and enriched (the Feast of the Navruz, which revives a beautiful spring in the soul of a person, the fast of the Eid, the sacrifice of the sacrifice and other folk holidays). In addition, it is time to delve into the history of our people, aesthetic culture and art, traditions and rituals. In such traditions, modernity is reflected in the artistic and aesthetic thinking of the Uzbek people as a world of sophistication, work on el-yurti, high feelings of ancestors.

The deep roots of the aesthetic culture of our people are formed by the teran veins of our past heritage and spirituality. Our modern national values are also developing, feeding on the ancient traditions and rituals of the peoples of Central Asia, enjoying mainly folk oral creativity, as well as fiction. They inherited from generation to generation and became rich on the basis of various ways of behavior, behavior in social life. The national traditions of the people, of which the unique and sérjilo is significant, are influencing cultural marriage with its antique manifestations in the development of aesthetic culture in social life. The delightful monotheism that is taking place among the people has always made folk customs, rituals and traditions colorful. Also, the role of social relations in the observance of the traditions of one ERA in the Society of the second period is incomparably greater. Basically, the educational significance of national-artistic values and traditions is more manifested in the proportion of production, in religious ceremonies, folk holidays.

Today, traditions are of great importance for the marriage of people, morality and folk rituals aesthetically in the upbringing of the younger generation, in the provision of spiritual feed.

The unique national traditions and values of our people are the main tools in the formation and upbringing of the aesthetic culture of the new century generation in maturing, energetic, graceful, graceful, beautiful, showy upbringing. National traditions will continue to be strengthened on the basis of achievements in the process of studying the nation, culture, lifestyle, literature and art. Especially on the basis of our traditions of national traditions, a rich aesthetic culture is closely connected with the world of sophistication and reflects aesthetic values in a unique way. In our traditions, such concepts as national spirit, dignity, latofat, femininity, ibo, sharm, Khayo come first. In this sense, our people, even in the context of globalization and modernization, focus on the history of their nation and operate aesthetically with high insight and intelligence, taste, emotion, ideals.

In the aesthetic culture of our people, maturing such qualities as nurturing their human and aesthetic feelings, loving people, dressing with Taste, always speaking sweetly, being humble and pure. Also, the national traditions of our country regarding many aesthetic cultures, such as "wedding ceremonies-cradle wedding, circumcision wedding, wedding wedding wedding, sayils-field sayli, flower sayli, melon sayli, procession, birthday celebration, boy bazmi, girl Assembly, visit parks, mass gathering and participation in performances"1 are the legacy of our wise ancestors. Using them wisely in perspective and making our marriage beautiful day by day is the main task for the younger generation. Therefore, everyone should look with respect for their people and the traditions of the whole world, live a comfortable and beautiful life, have a bright and beautiful world view, always strive to be a companion of a cheerful mood, constantly waving in the arms of a cheerful nature.

The fact that people know the universe and begin to perceive it aesthetically leads to the formation of national-artistic values. These values are an important factor in the enrichment of the human spiritual world, the feeling of the beauty of the outside world, the realization of spiritual processes that the eye does not progress. With the increase in national-artistic values in society, the pleasure attitudes of people towards the world of knowledge and sophistication change, and on the basis of modernization, a variety of visions, concepts, ideas begin to complicate. The newly emerging Milli-artistic value is directly connected with old values, demonstrating the influence of the world of spirituality in reality on the development of social and cultural ideals.

Even in a Global situation, aesthetic values serve to enrich the spiritual needs of people, their mafaats, financially living. Within the values, the highest value is considered human. For this reason, man strives to make Nature, Society and himself beautiful, beautiful, ugly, make the whole being his life good. In the process of globalization, a person of high value should not only get used to the world in one way, but also realize with his own consciousness such concepts in perspective as aesthetic culture, that is, good or bad, beautiful or ugly, fair or unadulterated. On this basis, it tries to sort out all the processes that will be divided into reality. In particular, a person is aware of dignity; begins with self-understanding. For this, first of all, aesthetic culture is considered of great importance in determining the life of a person, his fate. On the basis of aesthetic culture, a person is elevated as a high value. His activity, lifestyle will have a rich imagination of beauty and a comfortable life.

All changes in the field of aesthetic culture taking place in the socio-cultural life of Uzbekistan in the future are formed directly in connection with modern national and artistic values.

These values reflect human history in themselves and are an invaluable treasure in science and culture, cultural and domestic life, strengthening the family, forming feelings of sophistication towards nature, positively establishing Nations and National relations. There must be certain conditions and situations for the absorption of modern national and artistic values into the minds of those. It is in this case that values serve to make people decide on aesthetic views, cultural ideals, social ideas. No matter how much values are, they affect the spiritual maturity, aesthetic culture, National-spiritual needs of each nation. In particular, in today's globalization, the delightful attitude towards Uzbek dances, melodies, songs, which are a high example of aesthetic culture, is gaining positive importance. The current Uzbek dances, melodies, songs are not exactly what the classical cultural heritage is. these dances have become more modern, and they are noticeable in many aspects of European, Asian dance cultures. In this respect, we can see that the national-artistic values of the Uzbek people about the dance culture have long been enriched. But in essence, our dances largely retained the spirit of nationalism. These values all make people feel that their aesthetic culture is linked to history and that's how it always goes.

    As a result of the impact of globalization on

society, the aesthetic significance of national-artistic values in the individual and folk life increases, it can be seen that it is deeply studied by generations, and the latophobia and femininity of the past are also manifested in today's life. Because these values, forming the basis of aesthetic culture, Jeep people to each other, intertwine the beauty of the past and the sophistication of the future. Sometimes individuals are not able to realize that they are operating on aesthetic values. Even, the events of our Real life are intertwined with religious values.

Modern national and artistic values are an invaluable asset in increasing the aesthetic culture of our people. To keep them as eyebrows, to deliver them to the next generation, it is necessary to make all our capabilities, aesthetic feelings clear and neat. Therefore, today it is necessary to bring aesthetic culture in connection with values, enrich Enlightenment, culture and art with beautiful feelings, bring high and noble qualities to even higher heights in society.

Of great importance is the knowledge of the essence of modern national-artistic values, the belief in them, the maturation of aesthetic experiences on their basis, the absorption of national pride and feeling into the minds of the younger generation with all kinds of imagination. The aesthetic significance of values can also be traced back to past feelings of Valor and heroism. The future of educating young people on the basis of patriotism, commitment to duty, high culture, literature and art is the main goal of the great power. Moreover, the role of national and artistic values in improving the aesthetic education of young people is incomparably greater. The fact that everyone today knows their aesthetic values "honors humanity, places its dignity in place-it means restoring our national values, respecting our people with respect for their ancient and rich history, its traditions and Customs. The fact that only a person who is deeply aware of the heritage of his past can also be well versed in his national-artistic values has been highlighted by many allomas.

In general, in the process of globalization, national-artistic values are the decoration of a person's life, his point, the flower of his spirituality. In respect of these values in perspective, in delivering them aesthetically perfect and attractive to the younger generation, it is a pity that we adults do not always lose our vigilance.

Chapter Three. Language issues in the Uzbek mentality in Central Asia during globalization

3.1.§. The role of national values in the growth of youth moral culture in the era of globalization

In the new Uzbekistan, it has become an important process to educate the younger generation in full maturity, to strengthen the role of moral culture in reforms in the spiritual sphere, to bring up physically healthy and energetic, spiritually pure and conscientious, spiritually trigger and harmonious youth. It is an urgent matter of today to harmonize the lifestyle of young people with the moral traditions, images, rituals that have been formed for several centuries of our people, to educate them in every possible way as truly moral people. In the fulfillment of such a responsibility task, it is necessary that every citizen who has a child of this country, through his active citizenship position, manifests himself in the existing reality, creatively studies historical memory, realizes plans in perspective. The desire to deeply feel the opportunities and conditions created by the state in this regard, to enrich the moral culture of young people with elements of nationalism, has become an important socio-political reality of today.

It is positive that works related to the development of moral culture in society have increased in subsequent years. In our country, philosophers, moralists, cultural scientists and aestheticians created works on bringing spiritual life to a new level, raising youth education and moral culture, in which historical analysis of moral culture, development trends, features of manifestation in society are widely revealed. The study of theoretical and methodological issues of moral culture, the study of the level of spiritual maturity of young people in it, is considered an important philosophical process. Including A.As the lion advances his views on morality, "the fundamental essence of man is determined by the progressive development of oneself and one's own society. And morality never stands aside from this progress [64]". Indeed, morality is manifested through the nature of diverse people as a power that adorns a person's spiritual world, as a gift of his existence in existence.

As a fruit of youth support in the community, one can see the achievements that are

---

[64] Sher.A. Ethics. - Tashkent: 2007. P. 168.

being achieved today in science, art, literature, music, sports and many other fields. Because young people are the creators of our tomorrow, our future, which radiates high morality and decency into the world. The development of their moral culture, the education of modern thinkers is considered an important philosophical process. Because," in the context of current globalization, where our long-standing national values, the rules of etiquette inherited from our ancestors are at risk of complete disappearance, it is our primary task to focus on spirituality and Enlightenment, moral education on the desire of young people to acquire knowledge, to mature". To do this, it is always necessary to carry out the upbringing of the younger generation with Vigilance, Awareness, systematically controlling their moral culture.

The fundamental changes taking place in the socio-political image of the world are aimed at removing from the trail the moral culture and healthy lifestyle of both young people of New Uzbekistan in different ways. It is unfortunate that in relation to what is happening in social life, we all respond with vigilance and sensitivity to our high moral culture, to be aware of the way of life that is alien to us, which acquires a moral image in a new way. "Now there are more than 60 thousand sites on the internet that promote corruption, violence and immorality, "mass culture"[65]. How can we resist such sharp and complex information attacks and risks? What spiritual and spiritual feed are we giving young people through the Internet and social networks? Unfortunately, none of us can respond positively to this. As long as spiritual immunity to foreign ideas does not form in young people, it will be difficult to resist ideological risks, as long as the strict idea of "this is - good, this is – bad[66]" does not arise . It is advisable to avoid the negative impact of spiritual threats on the moral consciousness of young people, to be aware of various negative ideological views.

Since the issue of educating each young generation as a perfect person is considered a task in the first gal, in the process it is necessary to harmonize the moral culture of young people with the spirit of the times, to relate it to the heritage of our ancestors. While our people are distinguished

---

[65] Mirziyoev Sh.M. New Uzbekistan strategy. - Tashkent: Uzbekistan, 2021. Pp. 276-277.
[66] Mirziyoev Sh.M. From national recovery-towards national rise. - Tashkent: Volume 4, Uzbekistan, 2020. P. 178.

from other peoples by their tolerance and Oriental communalism, we should pay special attention to this issue morally in all aspects of our social life. Because, constantly negative situations such as" living according to the same habits, general principles, building on common values, obeying the same traditions and norms of morality, striving to uniformize the rules [67] " lead to a violation of the norms of moral culture. In such a situation, it is necessary to ensure that young people live in harmony with the times, but create conditions for the creative manifestation of their views, following the norm.

In the harmonious development of the moral culture of young people with national values, the formation of their spiritual world with historical memory, everyone should approach it responsibly. This condition, in turn, leads to the development of a healthy lifestyle of society, an increase in the role of vigilance in each activity. If this appearance does not arise, then we will have once again made sure how correct the transplant "the next regret is an enemy to yourself". It is necessary to realize that not only physical health,

---

[67] Kabylov Sh. Globalization and security. - Tashkent: IIB Academy of the Republic of Uzbekistan. 2006. P. 12.

but also the level of spiritual maturity plays a big role in the preparation of each parent's children for independent family life. We want young people to be happy in a healthy, free and prosperous homeland in every way, but we do not think that there are measures to achieve happiness, the importance of national values in the development of a moral culture that is a means for their spiritual upbringing to be healthy. National values are of great socio-educational importance in uniting our people, realizing feelings of self-realization and appreciation, exalting the moral and aesthetic culture of youth and society. This, in turn, serves to harmonize the spiritual and aesthetic culture of young people with modern national-artistic values, forming a new worldview and ideological image.

National-spiritual values, traditions, deeds, traditions and rituals are absorbed into the hearts and minds of young people through a temperate environment and a system of healthy upbringing, in which they form the characteristics of a national, social, moral-aesthetic mentality. The formation and development of youth on the basis of national-spiritual values is inextricably linked with the life, lifestyle, history, culture, customs, language, its past, future of the people "spiritual values are considered a great treasure in the first Gaul in the process of each state's understanding of its national identity. No state can imagine its bright future without developing and strengthening spiritual and aesthetic values in the minds of its people. For several thousand years now, the cultural values, spiritual heritage of the Uzbek people have been serving as a powerful source of spirituality for the peoples of the East, and, moreover, for the people of the whole world." Therefore, it is gratifying that today's children and the same youth as him have directly entered the development of the spiritual and moral sphere, conquering all spheres with their own achievements.

A human child can never grow up without upbringing in a way worthy of neither national nor universal values. As Abdullah Avlani said, "discipline is for us either a matter of life or life or salvation or destruction or happiness or disaster". Therefore, the continuous implementation of spirituality, moral culture with education is an urgent problem of this day. Because in the matter of Education, Parents and teachers in their activities should first see a person in the image of each child. Based on this requirement, it is darcor that the task of bringing young people to adulthood as perfect people with creative and broad thinking skills, who live consciously. Therefore, "we strive to preserve our spiritual life, our national consciousness and values, beliefs and thoughts, traditions and traditions , to raise our spiritual world," therefore, it is necessary to pay great attention to the educational system, form and Means.

Among the rich and unique, dissimilar and irreplaceable national-spiritual values of the Uzbek people, a special place is occupied by their delightful attitude to the spiritual education of young people. Developing on the basis of the family environment of young people, from childhood he sees the lifestyle of his parents and wants his life to be in the same spiritual way. Spiritual upbringing in the family environment carefully observes aspects, forms his own interest in life, matures his delightful attitudes towards reality. Spiritual upbringing in the family is more developed in girls on the basis of imitation of the mother, and in boys on the basis of imitation of the father. As the mother teaches her daughter a lesson, "a blanket sewn with a thread of love, a stretcher that sounded like a mother's heart song, a warm crib like a mother's hug, a doll with a girl's soul tongue, a" silk from a till" on the head of a child, a tray on a shelf, a tray, a tray on a throne, a crate

A person tries to make his moral culture beautiful in a monand way to his age, mind, career, life experience, ideal. Simply kitchen utensils-all kinds of trays, trays, pots, bowls, kettles, bowls, spoons, etc.serve not only to satisfy the need for a person's life, but also to beautify his life with a beautiful, spiritual and aesthetic culture.

In the field of religion, which today is the most delicate and complex, it should first be assumed that religion is one of the pillars of spirituality and moral culture, harmoniously developing with moral views in all times. Religion, in its essence, instills in the soul and mind of a person on the basis of spiritual education through such noble feelings as purity, kindness. We witness the growing conflict between goodness and evil in the world, along with the study, promotion of customs, rituals and holidays that have been formed over the centuries, passed down from generation to generation as an invaluable legacy.

Any moral culture will be viable, influential only if it takes into account the national traditions and lifestyle of the spiritual needs of the people. At the same time, in the process of globalization, the formation of national values in the minds of young people on the basis of moral culture in harmony with modernity is at the center of reforms. As a result of the work carried out in this area, it is necessary to instill in the minds of young people that nature, the state, society are needed not only to live free from various dangers, to leave offspring, but to unite with others, have high taste and wisdom, strive to build a free and prosperous homeland, cooperate and achieve the desired goals.

Today, such a historical opportunity has appeared before young people, critically evaluating the path taken by our ancestors, identifying the foundations of our statehood to the veins of our moral culture, finding the roots of our unexplored ancient heritage, imparting rich traditions of the past objectively to the young people of a new society, it is daunting every change taking place in

Currently, positive work is being carried

out in the fields of history, philosophy, spirituality, culture in order to raise the moral worldview of young people in New Uzbekistan. After all, a high moral culture and spirituality are the only way for citizens to give goodness, humanity, a radiant perspective. At the moment, one of the most important and serious problems of our state is the upbringing and upbringing of mature qualified young people. The future of the new Uzbekistan, its prospects, first of all, is the urgent task of an independent country to educate young people in a spiritual spirit, to grow them healthy, to form their minds free from the influence of the past. The transformation that is taking place in social life is instilled in the spirituality of young people, and the achievement of a high moral culture of our society is a requirement of the period.

At a time when the process of democratization of socio-spiritual and moral life in Uzbekistan is going on, youth respect universal values, deep knowledge of our spiritual heritage and history will serve for the prosperity of a free and prosperous homeland. More than ever, the importance of combining inner and outer beauty with morality has increased. Not only appearance in young people led to the fact that spiritual education is good, but also universal moral values began to be demanded from them, such as morally pure, rich in the spiritual world, generous, faithful, high in the culture of treatment.

There are also bad habits, bad agility and uneducated behaviors that negatively affect the moral culture of young people. From an early age, it is necessary to create a healthy socio-spiritual environment that will protect against such defects in the family, kindergarten, school and higher educational institutions. On the basis of morality, we must raise the culture of treatment in our language high on the basis of pleasure relationships, instill words that positively affect our psyche in the minds of our young people, promote that the purpose of living is to grow up to be a person of high spirituality. As long as a person lives, he will still feel the need for treatment, whether he wants it. Sweet and sincere treat, imaginative and diabolical, chaste and charming, polite, courageous, brave, alert and human, a person looks beautiful in the eyes of others both morally and aesthetically culturally. But people tastes are different. Because in people, taste can be good or bad, beautiful or ugly.

Morals of culture are not only the books that these people read, how much the cinema they see or the clothes they wear, but also the purity and height of consciousness and understanding.

The consciousness of young people in the new Uzbekistan is developed on the basis of a number of socio-spiritual factors based on moral and national values:

- the manifestation of youth in its social appearance, that is, in its dependence on spiritual and moral and aesthetic appearance, culture and improvement;

- the spiritual education of society and the individual is progressive in their dialectical connection. While democratic reforms in society play a primary role in the formation of personality spirituality, in turn, the spiritual education of young people is of great importance in the development of society spirituality;

- in the absorption of ideas of independence into the minds of young people, spiritual education and morality become a powerful spiritual factor that brings to the human soul the spirit of freedom and creativity, based on the meaning and essence of modernity;

- spiritual education, at the same place, is

the spiritual strength of youth in their pursuit of a healthy lifestyle and perfection.

In New Uzbekistan, it is gratifying for all that yoshar honors national values and practices in his activities. But there is also a low cultural-spiritual level of some. Therefore, it is imperative to enrich the moral culture of young people in all areas with a fundamentally new image, increase their attention to nationalism. The maturation of the education and spiritual worldview of the younger generation on the basis of national values has been and remains an inextricable process in society. This situation can be seen in the image of young people entering the spiritual and moral spheres of society.

The development of the moral culture of young people in society as an inextricable process is carried out in parallel with historical consciousness. In this activity, it is considered important to bring young people to adulthood in the spirit of national values and the formation of folk moral thinking. It is necessary to strengthen in every way the moral attitude of young people towards reality in social life, to live freely and comfortably in jaimism. Today, in our social life, cities and villages corresponding to the youth lifestyle are developing and gaining expression in the media, literature and art. Therefore, since we pay great attention to the upbringing of our youth in the spirit of national values, we cannot forget that their activities have expanded into all spiritual and moral spheres, especially since the achievements in the fields of Science, Education and culture are important to serve the prosperity of our country. Along the way, it will be an important process to unite our youth with one maslak, to strengthen high respect for national values.

3.2.§. Philosophical foundations of the development of aesthetic culture in society

The emergence of many masterpieces of spirituality in the process of the development of human history is directly related to the patterns of aesthetic culture, which do not directly affect the social lifestyle of the growing younger generation. The ANA'ana and rituals of such appearance enrich their image between periods on the basis of philosophical views in society. On the basis of these, the aesthetic culture of each person "covers such areas as spiritual-cultural life, educational upbringing, cultural heritage, historical experience, religious, moral, educational views, lifestyle, colorful relationships, science, folk holidays, parties, performances and events, art, literature.[68]" This development of attractive and unique spaces of aesthetic culture is a product of the democratic reforms carried out in society, in which the national-cultural values, which are considered dear to each individual, serve to demonstrate the spiritual world of the new Uzbekistan with their

---

[68] Musaev F. Philosophical and legal foundations of building a Democratic state. - Tashkent: "Uzbekistan", 2007. P. 119.

universal and humanism. As a result of this, the national democratic changes carried out in society, on the other hand, support the traditions of the people, their values formed in the process of socio-historical development, encourage them to preserve as national-cultural wealth, to use them more efficiently in the formation of a new generation. In which country, no matter what social space it is realized, literal democracy cannot reject Ana'anawi values under the banner of modernization, changes that do not rely on evolutionism do not take place in the people's way of life, in the heart.

In order for a person to mature in our society in every possible way, it is imperative that we pay special attention to the ANA'anas, national values, udum and rituals, which form the basis of religious and secular knowledge that was formed before, historically. This assumes that everyone relies on objective and subjective factors in society. These factors always require that" in the context of current globalization, where our long-standing national values, the rules of etiquette inherited from our ancestors, are at risk of complete disappearance, it is our primary task to focus on spirituality and Enlightenment, moral education, the desire to acquire knowledge, to mature". The development of national values in society directly serves the rise of a specific national worldview and aesthetic culture.

When analyzing the philosophical foundations of aesthetic culture in society, it will be necessary to focus on aspects of its connection with the process of historical progress, to study what the world of spirituality was, reflected in folk thought, to take into account historical conditions. At the moment, it has become the task of society to create an era in which each person realizes his own, understands changes in the field of aesthetic culture with high spirituality. This requires the creation of a non-exclusive program and laws aimed at the bright prospect of a new Uzbekistan, the consistency of reforms in social life, and at the same time it is being implemented in all areas of society in stages.

The new image of the aesthetic culture taking place in our society indicates that reforms serve the value of a person, the rich and thoughtful development of democratic principles indicates that the goal of the spiritual world is a person with high spirituality. The absorption of the tag-stem of this activity into the spiritual world of a person, enriched with masterpieces of aesthetic culture, should make it a masterpiece of beauty. Today, in the formation and development of aesthetic culture, "there is no rich and unique moral-spiritual, spiritual-aesthetic golden heritage-a more reliable source than habits, images, traditions." Because for all these centuries, his plausible and aesthetically flamboyant character has always exceeded his dignity with the inclusion of Sergio Fayz in the aesthetic vision of the individual. As the heirs of a new society, we must always preserve the masterpieces of aesthetic thinking higher than this, deliver them in their own way to future generations, introduce rare manuscripts and works of aesthetic culture created by our ancestors to the whole world, demonstrate how rich and attractive our past has always been moving forward in the field of Science and culture.

The development of philosophical thought brings up individuals with a unique and appropriate modern worldview for each period, providing an impetus for the development of society on the basis of a new social environment. In this process, the role of aesthetic culture is strong in the philosophical worldview system, which brings the prospect of the people to a high peak, and a national ideology is formed that takes on a special appearance in the way of the fate of the nation, the prosperity of the Motherland, the peace of the land, the well-being of the people. As its driving force, the main role should be played by the social relations between the individual and the state, the approach to reality from an aesthetic point of view, the motivation of people towards aesthetic culture.

Starting from the early days of civil society being built in the new Uzbekistan, the question of the formation of nationalism, the restoration of national values began to find its bright expression in the system of social relations. In such a context, every society felt the need for a philosophical worldview aimed at forming the national feelings of a person, serving for the individual and society, raising the fate of the people to the level of a high aesthetic culture. As a result, the prosperity of society and the emergence of an aesthetic culture, which embodied the long-standing aspirations of the people, aimed at exalting the aesthetic culture of the individual, led to its importance.

It is relevant to prioritize human interests in

the civil society being built in the new Uzbekistan, to strengthen the state's activities in the process of reform more and more in the way of human dignity. According to the laws of Social Development, "the idea and ideology and culture of a person are decisive in society." It is in this activity that the need of society for citizens with high tastes increases. This, in turn, requires a strong formation of a certain idea or ideology in all areas of social life, directing people who are becoming the driving force of society towards noble goals. As a result, a philosophical worldview is formed, consisting of the sum of certain views and thoughts that reflect the lifestyle of the people, a common-minded person or a person. This process always serves as a power divider for spiritual and spiritual processes, calling people to high heights on the basis of aesthetic ideals.

The main philosophical roots of aesthetic culture are formed by universal values in World Philosophy, Eastern philosophy and the philosophical views of our allomas grown from our country. The material and spiritual heritage of each individual and nation, which has been formed in the worldview of humans for thousands of years and passed down from ancestors to generations, has manifested an aesthetic culture in itself.

The opportunity to realize the National specific aspects of aesthetic culture has expanded in New Uzbekistan, along with creating a social environment for the free survival and development of a person in society. As a result, special attention was paid to the development of historical spiritual and aesthetic values, changing the attitude towards values close to the hearts of our people. In social life, the need arose for the continuous growth of the aesthetic consciousness of a person, the perfect study of the heritage of his great ancestors, the widespread study of their names. After all, the stabilization of the political, economic and spiritual and aesthetic foundation of the new Uzbekistan is inextricably linked with the hard work, spiritual perfection, development of aesthetic culture, rise of legal consciousness, non-dependence on other forces of each individual. This has a direct impact on the rise of aesthetic culture in society. In the renewal and development of the new Uzbekistan, the impact of the "development strategy"on economic, social, artistic and aesthetic processes has been great, leading to a change, renewal and development of people's consciousness and thinking. It became a new and modern reform, which expressed not only the national and universal characteristics of the aesthetic culture of the individual, the socio-historical experience of the country, but also the social practice of artistic creativity and aesthetic attitude to reality.

In the 21st century, humanity has reached such a period that the more any national limitation harms its spiritual life, the more respect and attention to any, national and universal values serve the National-Spiritual rise. To date, this thing has led to the manifestation of its dangerous aspects in the activities of some individuals. Under the ulterior motives of such individuals, it can be observed that "the century-old values of the nation, national thought and lifestyle are being traced, morality, family and community life, conscious lifestyle are seriously endangered." This further expanded the social needs and capabilities of the individual as a shell protecting our people from various dangers. Our people were able to directly perceive the material and spiritual resources created and created by other peoples and states, to know the innovations in the field of

Science, Technology and culture. This freedom, in turn, also led to the formation and development of a new aesthetic culture. Since aesthetic culture, by its nature, prospered thanks to the aesthetic values that people are revered by all mankind, dear and necessary to all mankind, today it has created such a social environment and historical conditions.

One of the main socio-philosophical issues in the formation and development of a new aesthetic culture was the attitude to the spiritual heritage of the people, its strengthening and development. This issue was a huge socio-historical, ideological-philosophical problem. Because modern life cannot be achieved without properly addressing issues of spirituality, without shaping the people's correct attitudes towards history and modern life. Because when it comes to spirituality, referring to our cultural heritage, tradition and painting, religious values, language and literature, art and historical memories, all these listed social phenomena are fundamental aspects that make up the form and content of aesthetic culture.

Aesthetic culture cannot be imagined without objective and subjective factors such as national language and its problems, historical memory and painting, beauty of the land and moral values, etc. The wider and more diverse aesthetic culture contains objective and subjective factors, the wider and more vast the aesthetic values are, the universe is. All things and phenomena that make up the concept of aesthetic values also constitute the content and essence of aesthetic culture. When we think deeply about the structural factors that make up these aesthetic values, we make sure that all these factors serve as a key factor in how much aesthetic culture is formed and developed.

Since the life of a person passes in the environment of his people, people, nation and country, his relationship and communication with people occurs through his native language, historical memory, painting and religious values take place from the spirituality of a person, since a human child is associated and associated with his parents, relatives, neighbors, such social relations are sealed by imagination and feelings such as loyalty, respect, trust, conscience and freedom,

The formation and development of such national, universal qualities ultimately represents spiritual perfection, in particular, the development of aesthetic culture. The development of aesthetic thinking in turn also fosters a sense of respect and appreciation for the culture and spirituality of other peoples and countries. Aesthetic culture has social significance as a means of honoring, enjoying, and also showing significance to universal common aspects in peoples ' spirituality. Spirituality, in particular, aesthetic culture and aesthetic thinking are not a manifestation of Destiny. It is formed, developed through mental and physical labor, through the historically formed and modern system of education of the nation, enlightenment and the attitude to life with a pure conscience and devotion.

The result of the upbringing of aesthetic culture in a person is that a person is confident in his strength, a person is satisfied with what he is doing, the craft he is doing, stability is created in the form of a person. A person with a high aesthetic culture does not give in to the fleeting kayfu Safo, does not strive to build his marriage through a light path, does not follow destructive ideas. Because aesthetic culture is an expression of an elegant sensory perception that calls on individuals, humanity to unite in the world of beauty and creativity with its social essence.

Since aesthetic culture depends primarily on the emotional world of the individual, external and internal influences and impressions, it is also a necessary social task to develop a clear system of the direction of objective and subjective factors. This national identity will be of great importance in determining the place and position of this country, this nation among the peoples of the world.

In the following years, great attention is paid to the upbringing of each individual in the spirit of love for the motherland, loyalty to the heritage of our ancestors, ideas of independence and patriotism. To do this, a new socio-aesthetic environment is first being built in order to re-transform the places where the human eye falls, living life, educational and working conditions, and to form a new aesthetic culture. This aesthetic activity pays off not only in education, but also in our villages, which make up the main part of our people. Because the High example of this aesthetic culture was inherited by our ancestors.

Such feelings express the features of aesthetic experiences, aesthetic culture, aesthetic thinking. Since aesthetic forgiveness is watered with the spirit of creativity, beauty and humanity, the higher the social significance of the results of human labor as a result of it. Therefore, it is necessary to relate to the increasingly beautiful nature of the new Uzbekistan and to individuals who are the first to accept changes in people's lives and feel responsible for these changes.

Today, conditions have arisen in society for the release and upbringing of such qualities. In the upbringing of people in the national spirit, commonality arose in the interests and tasks of the individual, family and society. At the same time, parents and society were given very large tasks and responsibilities. A person with a wide range of thinking, a deep education and enlightenment about man and humanity can only mobilize all his mental and spiritual capabilities in the path of fate and prosperity of his nation and country, delight in every achievement of his people and country and suffer from defects and mistakes that undermine progress. And the sum of such experiences becomes socialized as a result of a new aesthetic culture, thinking and worldview.

In the center of further socio-spiritual reforms in society, the issue of raising a harmonious generation has become a nationwide,

nationwide task. The prospect of our country, the issue of creating a free and comfortable life, the role and position that Uzbekistan occupies in the world community in the 21st century depends on how the younger generation is formed as a person. If they are properly brought up, their new thinking, their spiritual world is deeply immersed in national and universal values, and all their material and spiritual needs for aesthetic culture are taken into account in a timely manner, the intellectual potential of our state and country will be so enhanced. Taking into account the fact that each individual, by his nature, will be curious about everything, follow the good and the bad and succumb to various influences, taking into account his age, circle of interest and abilities will give a positive result.

In general, aesthetic culture does not decide as a pure spiritual derivative of a person's moral, religious, legal, scientific, artistic and practical need, desire, aspirations. Aesthetic culture is embodied as a general and common expression of all sides of the consciousness and soul of a person. Therefore, the integration of the individual with members of society in the pursuit of noble goals and the desire to live in the social environment with the requirements of healthy living, in its essence, makes it necessary to take the formation and development of aesthetic culture seriously.

3.3. §. Processes of development of language and philosophical views on the land of Central Asia

In the history of the personality society, the territory of Central Asia has attracted world peoples as the basis of the development of the Turkic language, in which specific cultures and values are formed. This area is considered a place of cultural life, where the literary heritage of our people, ideological views are embodied, one of the first jets of spirituality, the ground on which socio-philosophical ideas arose. It embodied the literature created on language and philosophy at different times, the images of heroes in works based on Real reality, the expression of philosophical thought in literary genres in our national culture. In them, the reflection of the processes of formation of language and philosophical views on the basis of values for centuries in the hearts of the younger generation, the manifestation of the national image of the ideas of goodness and justice in our history[69].

The Central Asian region, as a settlement

---

[69] Mirziyoev Sh.M. New Uzbekistan strategy. - Tashkent: Uzbekistan, 2021. Pp. 35-36.

where a rich intellectual potential has long been formed, is characterized by rich philosophical masterpieces of our ancestors, ancient oral and written sources, narratives that reflect the image of national heroes, traditions that have merged with the ground. Of particular importance in them is the way of life, art, culture of Turkic peoples, the world of philosophical thought, a subtle aesthetic worldview, moral values of the FAQ from other peoples. The harmonization of Turkic language-based ideas formed on this land with diiny beliefs, views with the creation of being, ground and heaven in the "Avesto"are elements of a specific philosophical thought. The unity of the noble word, the noble thought and the noble deed in this work is considered the main idea in ensuring the eternity of life, in enriching the immortality of language. The processes of parallel development of philosophical views in Central Asia with language have not only served as the basis for later periods, but also contributed to the development of spiritual treasures in the world[70].

Although in the history of mankind, language has always been a means of communication for humans, but its processes of

---

[70] Philosophy qomusiy logat. - Tashkent: East, 2004. P. 399.

development in society have directly represented specific philosophical aspects. Despite its presence in different dialects, its continuous use in the Daily way of life for humans has always given rise to the unity of cultures and values. "The enlightened people who respect their language also have a deep respect for the language of others. In this regard, our great-grandfathers showed signs and examples. In particular, our great-ancestors, such as Muhammad Khwarazmiy, Imam Bukhari, Imam Termiziy, Ahmad Farghani, Abu Nasr Farabi, Abu Rayhun Beruniy, Abu Ali ibn Sino, Mahmud Zamakhshari, Alisher Navoi, have conquered the heights of world science even for their thorough knowledge of dozens of languages" . It is noteworthy that in their time they worked in dozens of languages and created their own unique works in the field of Science, served the rise of the philosophical consciousness and worldview of the people.

The philosophical views of Central Asia, formed from time immemorial, reflect the national mentality, moral ideals, ideological ideas of the people. This process has been renewed for centuries and has shown its positive influence on the development of the language between certain periods. "Science, as a result of the study of the historical stages of development of the human language, came to the conclusion that language as a means of Communication, Speech, is undoubtedly only a product of the human brain." These aspects have served to honor a person in society as a high value, to mature on the basis of modern knowledge. That is why the history of Central Asia has served for centuries for the prospect of science. Its rich culture, sa'nati, moral ideals, spiritual heritage are harmonized with the masterpieces of philosophical thought of our ancestors.

From time immemorial, Central Asia had its own linguistic and philosophical thinking, based on the ideology of that time. The roots of great science and culture go back to the distant past, and these are the monuments called the O'hun-Enasoy Scrolls. The O'rhun-Enasoi scrolls are an early example of books inscribed on large stones, namely literary and philosophical assars.

During the Arab invasions, the Somonian period, several more groups of Iranians migrate to Khwarezm, and they also settle in a compact way. From the time of the Achaemenids, Persian,

Aramaic words begin to enter the khwarezmian language of khohna Oghuz, which we can observe in all Turonian regions. Living in a highly recorded compact form, Iranian neighborhoods are intermingled with the Iranian people as the ages pass, who lose their language and begin to speak Khwarezmian, i.e. Turkic. Representatives of the Indo-European approach spread this situation throughout Khwarezmia, arguing that the supposedly old Khwarezmian language, that is, Eastern Iranian, has become a dead language, while the Khwarezmian people have become Turkified Persians.

In the world, dead languages are many shulir, etusk, Latin are dead languages, a phenomenon often explained by assimilation or the complete scraping of Ethnos. In Turan, in particular in Khorezm, neither unisi nor this happened. Because the Medes and Persians lived in Iran, India, Central Asia, Egypt, Asia Minor at that time, 18 million. assimilation of the population could not do either, it did not have the strength or resources to completely subjugate them. On top of this, Khwarazm is located very far from the Achaemenid Kingdom, which in order to get to it will have to travel hundreds of kilometers of the Karakum Desert. The conclusion is that the khwarazmians were one of the oldest Turkic language, the oghiz-speaking autotkhan Ethnos, and still live today.

From the oasis of Khorezm to the Zarafshan Basin, we move to the ancient sugary space. Manifestations of the Indo-European approach also consider sughdians to be Eastern Iranian speaking Persians. Let's look at how true or wrong this idea is based on sources. According to the famous muarrix Narshahi, author of the"history of Bukhara", "in Samarkand there was a river called" Nasaf Darya " (Zarafshan River), which collected a lot of water, pushed the mud, resulting in a swamp. The flooding then stopped. The settlement of Bukhara gradually overflowed into flat land, and thus it became a Big River Sugd, and the subject of this turbidity remained Bukhara: "people from all sides gathered and this place became prosperous." This historical record testifies to the fact that Central Asia has long been a multilingual region.

In the old Turkic language, these literary works, written in a specific letter, were created in the 6th-8th centuries. It embodied the ideas expressed by the Turkic peoples ' love for their elu-land, their heroism, their resentment against foreign invaders. Having traveled through the lands inhabited by the Turkic peoples of Central Asia and its environs, ulugolim Mahmud Qoshgari described his views on the language, history, way of life, philosophy, ideas in the artistic work of the Turkic peoples of ancient times in his book "The Lord of Turkic words" ("Devonu lexicatit turk"), which he completed in 1069. Shortly after its creation, in 1069-1070, Joseph khosz Khojib of Bolasagun wrote his epic "Qutadgü bilig", ("the knowledge that brings good"), in which he expresses his moral, educational thoughts in an attractive, artistic form, advancing the ideas of goodness, righteousness and popularism. The O'hun-Enasoy Scrolls promoted heroic, patriotic, and humanistic ideas, and the boonyuk, slave tigin, Bilga hoqon, Ungin, Moyun Chur scrolls are considered O'hun scrolls, while the Eletmish Bilga hoqon, uyuq Tarlaq, uyuq Turan, Elegesh, Begra, chakol, Achur, Oltinkol, Uybat memorabilia are scrolls found in Enasoy. Legal documents, covenants, marriage contracts, sale documents, correspondence between the rulers of Sogdians, Shosh, Turks and Ferganas, documents on the daily life of the farm and decrees of various contents in Sogdian, dating from the 4th-10th centuries were found in Central Asia. These documents were found in Mugqal'a in Sughdiyona, Afrosiyob Hill in Samarkand, Kyrgyzstan and Eastern Turkestan. Arabic-language sources covering the medieval history of Central Asia include the 8th-9th century Arab historian Abulhasan Ali ibn Muhammad al-Madoini's "Akhbor al-Khulafo" ("history of the caliphs"), "Historia al-buldon" ("history of the lands"), the 9th century major geographer and historian scholar Al-Ya'qubi's "Kitab al-buldon" ("book of the lands"), and "Historia". Sources in 9th-century Arabic also include literary works by Abubakr Ahmad ibn Yahya jabir al-Balazuri, such as "Kitab futux al-buldon" ("a book on the conquest of the lands") and "Kitab ansob al-sharaf" ("a book on the genealogy of the noble"). Medieval Arabic sources can also include the works of Abu Yusuf Ya'qub, Ibn al-Faqih, Ibn Khurdadbeh, Tabariy, Ahmad ibn Fadlan, Al-Ma'sudiy, Abulfaraj Qudama, Istakhriy, Ibn Hawqal, Abu Dulaf, Al-Holy, Utbiy, As-Saolibi. When the works of these authors provide information about the regions where Islam is spread, the issues of the States located in

Movarounnahr and Khurosan, their socio-economic and cultural-spiritual development are also highlighted. The works of the authors about the way of life of Central Asia, the processes associated with the socio-spiritual world are today considered a kind of treasure and source of knowledge for the upbringing of the younger generation.

The roots of the culture and spirituality, language and philosophical views of our people are intertwined with an incredibly rich history. On the issue of its antiquity and strong foundation, the existence of an energetic spiritual world of many ancient States on this land, President Shavkat Mirziyoyev pays special attention to his works, lectures, conversations. Speaking about such projects that are an important event in our spiritual life, it is necessary to note the beginning of work on establishing the activities of scientific and educational institutions such as the center of Islamic civilization in Uzbekistan, international research centers in the names of Imam Bukhari and Imam Termiziy, Islamic Academy, president of Uzbekistan Shavkat Mirziyoev, among them special schools for the study of religious and educational Of course, these works of ours have a deep scientific and practical basis . These aspects serve to discredit a specific philosophical worldview in the upbringing of the younger generation, in the study of the history of Central Asia.

The fact that the territory of Central Asia has long been a place of high spirituality and enlightenment, the socio-economic foundations of statehood that arose in it are considered a breakthrough for all of us. The unique artifacts created by our ancestors, the masterpieces of national values and spirituality that have been passed down from ancestors to generations for centuries, are our unique assets. Within them, the presence of hundreds of works on philosophy, hanfasa, logic, history, ethics and spirituality will strengthen the entire world community's interest in it. We need to study these achievements of our people through today's scientific research, to convey to future generations their wisdom about the science of enlightenment and politics in them.

- Analysis and Results (Analysis and results). The foundation of language and philosophy, formed on the territory of Central Asia, has strong, energetic roots, the stages of its development have preserved itself in any conditions. Many masterpieces of spiritual heritage created by our ancestors, spiritual, moral, philosophical, political and legal works, samples of philosophical thought, achievements of science are based on the scientific conclusions that arose on this point, relying and ensuring the vitality of the national language.

Of particular importance in Central Asia has long been the role of our ancestors in the development of socio-philosophical ideas in the development of science. Their works related to philosophy and language have served as treasures of spirituality for humanity. First President Of The Republic Of Uzbekistan I.A. As Karimov noted, " how many centuries our ancestors have lived in this vast region in harmony and on what values, while it is still permissible today, history and the flange of life, nature itself challenges us – all the peoples of Central Asia-to live life in the spirit of just such friendship and cooperation. In a word, this is how you look at historical reality, the feeling of living as a jamuljam has become for us a philosophy of life, and even more precisely, a rule of life. In modern language, it is such a feature that forms the basis of our national mentality, distinguishing us from others, that it is not at all possible not to notice, not to realize, not to see it." This, in turn, created wide conditions for the stabilization of the peace of the land and the well-being of the people, the centuries-old veneration of universal culture and spirituality, the joint harmonious development of philosophical thought and language. The ground has witnessed the centuries-old people speak a wide variety of languages, live with each other in harmony and Grace.

As a result of the adoption of many regulatory documents in the following years on the development of Social Sciences in society, it also opened the door to wide opportunities for the study of foreign languages. For the knowledge of each younger generation, a thorough understanding of the task that language fulfills in society, in which the development through language of perfection of the spirit of loyalty to the motherland, patriotism, loyalty to the National idea was deeply analyzed. Of particular importance is the efforts of the head of state to consistently establish work in this regard. In particular, the decree of F-5465 "on measures to develop a concept for the development of a national idea at a new stage of development of

Uzbekistan", adopted on April 8, 2019, forms a special attitude of tolerance in their pursuit of one goal, despite the fact that different nationalities and nationalities living in society speak different languages. One of the most important factors in our country is the fact that the principle of cooperation between different categories of people, political forces and parties, interethnic harmony, interreligious tolerance is studied in the spirit of today's times through the Social Sciences. The ideology of the period expresses the importance of the fact that more than 130 nationalities and elat people live in Uzbekistan and a new philosophical worldview has been formed in their minds in relation to the National idea, the role of Social Sciences in the educational system in improving human knowledge in this regard. This is a sign that there have been no national conflicts between citizens for centuries and that our people serve the development of Science in mutual harmony on the basis of long-standing tolerance.

  The spiritual foundation of our people, the foundations of our state are very ancient and strong, which no one can deny. How many millennia have our history gone by, in the historical development of our people, the foundations of statehood have been established in many languages, science, culture have developed. The National idea of our people, the national ideology rich historical spiritual heritage, the national and universal values of our people have developed on the basis of these languages. Religious values have their influence on the national mentality, customs, traditions and traditions, and the system of ideas arising from the content and essence of the main idea of the Turkic language is valid in the life of society both in our history and today. The development of such a high philosophical thought directly embodied representatives of different nationalities as a kind of hearth of Science, a place of enlightenment for the peoples of Central Asia.

Thoughts, views and ideas that serve as a basis, a basis for our national ideology, have a Turkic language and historical basis in our country, and views on the spirituality and enlightenment of the peoples of our region have been formed in stages in our historical development. In Civilization, which originated on the territory of Central Asia, Turkic is considered one of the most ancient languages in the world.

That is why this language has its own philosophical foundations and played the main role in the lifestyle of the peoples of the same region, in the culture of communication. Production in the region, international trade relations, intercultural dialogues, science, madanicht, art, among others, all served for the development of the language and the civilization of the peoples of the East.

Historically, our ancestors who lived in khududud, called Turan, Movarounnahr, Turkestan, have been creating literary works in the Turkic language for centuries, creating and coming Asori-atiqas, fairy tales and legends, Thermae, epics, proverbs and sayals, songs and lapars that perform at weddings and parties, Games, festivals and trips, culture and spirituality, jamiki legacies related to enlightenment, customs, traditions and traditions serve as sources for the formation and development of the national ideology. One of the oldest types and genres of oral creativity of our people, the myth and asothers put forward the idea of good vs. evil, light vs. darkness, happiness vs. misfortune, and the triumph of goodness over evil in this struggle. The "Avesto", the Holy Book of Zoroastrianism, notes that the one God who created and ruled the universe, Ahura – Mazda, calls on people to fight for goodness, he gives light, heat, happiness to people as the Lord of good deeds, saves people from troubles, makes his musk easy. The goddess of evil, Achriman, however, distracts people from the right path, leading them to evil. The forces of evil and darkness in the folklore of the peoples of the East are often depicted in myths in the form of giant dragons and demons. They are manifested as symbols of disaster and darkness, misfortune and disgrace, death and calamity, misfortune, homelessness, hunger. At the heart of these views, the philosophical worldview of man in relation to life expands, and his social ideals are polished. His philosophical consciousness about language, with its unique facets, exerts its influence on the development of society.

Our literary heritage, which has arisen over several centuries in our region, has been described in the epics "Tomaris", "Shiroq", "Zariadr and Odiq", "Zarina and Striangia", "Manas", "Alpomish", "Qirqqiz", "Gooroglu", "Avazkhan", "chambil qamali", "Oysuluv" as examples of heroism for the liberation and independence of our Motherland, the ideas of national philosophical and universal importance about patriotism in these works for its ideology, the tag serves as the ground and basis.

The doctrine, attitude and ideas on the need to defend the motherland, the freedom of the motherland, the blood of the navel, the land preserved and venerated by the ancestors as an eyebrow, the need to selflessly defend the motherland are prominent in all examples of folk oral and written creativity. Patriotism is a quality of high humanity inherent in all people who have connected their fate with the fate of the Motherland, the nation, who are devoted to the path of tomorrow's perspective. The possibilities, fame, prestige of the country, the development of the nation will also be associated with the level of patriotic feelings of people of this nationality. Such a philosophical worldview has long served for the independence, freedom and freedom of each people.

For our ancestors, descendants, ancestors, love for the motherland, Eli, was a sacred feeling. They put above all the question of the Fatherland, the interest of the People, national dignity, dignity, dignity, as an honor for themselves to sacrifice their lives, their lives, in the cause of these interests when necessary. That is why the more understanding of the interests, dignity, fate, prospects of the Motherland, the higher the sense of patriotism in people. This process is endless. Various stages of historical, socio-political, spiritual progress discover new and new facets of patriotism. Today, citizens of new Uzbekistan are also brought up as patriotic people, along with their views and spiritual wealth. They are moving towards tomorrow's progress in solidarity for the development of their native languages.

Calling on all peoples to live in friendship, morality, hand-to-hand, maximalism, Semitism, subversion of national separatism, calling to live with thought of perspective, categorically condemning betrayal of ancestral oaths, national deeds, instructions, living and functioning with the thought of the happiness and prospect of their children, being faithful to love for a lifetime, and other similar universal ideas are common aspects characteristic of the culture, ideology of

As the historical basis and source of the National idea and ideology, the rules that are important for the national ideology in the "Avesto"consist in overcoming the given word, staying faithful to it, strictly adhering to trade and contracts, paying off the debt on time, free from deception and betrayal, faithfulness.

The universe in "Avesto" consists of an uncompromising struggle between Akhuramazda and Akhriman, the symbols of the forces of goodness and evil, while in Akhuramaz, seeking to establish good, justice, prosperity, peace, in the world, Akhriman leads people to evil, darkness, death, destruction. In this struggle, confident people strive to stand by Akhuramazda. The idea that goodness triumphs over evil in the struggle between good and evil, light and darkness, happiness and misfortune is the main idea in "Avesto". "Avesto" is an important source of the past history, culture, spirituality and thought of our ancestors, national idea and ideology.

Samples of spiritual culture, which embodied the intelligence and thinking, manners, culture, spirituality, enlightenment, rich life experiences of the peoples of ancient Central Asia, were manifested through Turkic language. From time immemorial, Central Asian allomas were those who read and studied the monuments of spirituality created by the peoples of medieval Turkestan and mastered their basic ideas. In this way they formed spiritual and moral values in themselves, such as morality, goodness, humanity. The cultural heritage, decency, educational traditions of our people, the National idea and ideology of the peoples of Uzbekistan, formed over the centuries, show deep historical roots. At the heart of this lies the strong will of the people, the native language, which has developed over the centuries. It is a fear that we will further strengthen the role of this language in society and enrich its universally accepted aspects.

Ideological, ideological foundations of the development of Uzbekistan national-spiritual way of life and thinking of the population, folk traditions and Customs based on the Turkic language, respect for adults inherent in the national mentality and spirituality of the Uzbek people, care for family and Children, Open volunteering, benevolence towards people regardless of their nationality and a sense of mutual assistance are important aspects in ideological, ideological The issues of love and love for the motherland, hard work, striving for knowledge, enlightenment, the formation and elevation of feelings of national pride and pride in citizens are important tasks of national ideology and ideology. In our historical spiritual heritage, the main attention was paid to these issues and a lot of attention was paid to the upbringing of spirituality in the conduct of ideological and ideological education.

The language, culture, morality, moral views, philosophy of the peoples of Central Asia serve to educate today's younger generation in the spirit of national values. The spirituality of the people is directly related to the past of the nation and its foundation, making it rich by taking food from the achievements of the science created by the ancestors. The role of language in this is great, and the education and upbringing of our children today, the next day of our people, depends on this spiritual heritage. Because the path to the human soul is first given through language. "There is also an affinity in the fields of philosophy and Linguistics with regard to problem research. The roots of such a connection have a long history. In particular, the human problem occupies a fundamental place in philosophy and Linguistics, since its feedback is materialized directly through language.[71]" From such a simple requirement, it is

---

[71] Bozorov M.J. From the history of the stages of the development of linguofalsafa // problems of philosophy and methodology of the sciences. - Tashkent: Institute of philosophy and law, 2011. P. 38.

our main goal to educate those who have the ability to think independently and broadly through language. We are all responsible for bringing to adulthood those Spiritualized individuals who live consciously in society, embody in themselves the qualities inherent in the glory of man. Today, the main goal and task of each parent should be to ensure the access of their child to communication through different languages. It is required that every parent, mentor and Coach approach this work with an incredibly great sense of responsibility. Why do we say that our citizens are worthy owners of folk spirituality. Along this path, we must all come together and develop the pandemics and exhortations of our ancestors through the eternity of our language.

Conclusion

All socio-political and spiritual reforms carried out in Uzbekistan were built on the basis of human interests. A new system of Education has been developed and is being implemented in stages in order to bring to adulthood a harmonious generation of Thinking, Creating at the level of World templates, with the provision of such qualities as our national-cultural heritage, Oriental traditions of morality, humanity, patriotism, tolerance inherent in our national mentality.

On the basis of our traditional, spiritual, scientific, aesthetic and moral values, the restoration of the spirit of the individual, the formation of his consciousness became the main task. Reforms in the spiritual sphere were carried out in three closely related directions: spiritual restoration, spiritual purification and spiritual elevation.

Particular attention was paid to the fact that spiritual education was not carried out without the problems of spirituality and enlightenment. The high morale of an enlightened person was taken as the basis for a new educational system. Thus, great importance was placed on the social unity and connection between upbringing and upbringing, the environment and the individual, the individual and society.

In the system of upbringing, special attention was paid to spiritual education. Morality was perceived as a mirror of a person's social ideal and attitude to society, not just an expression of a culture of treatment.

Hence, spiritual recovery is associated with higher culture, and aesthetic culture is an important factor in leading to moral perfection.

Spiritual recovery means understanding, respecting the heritage of ancestors, honoring the blessings of independence, continuing Oriental Customs and traditions, worrying about the love and prospect of the motherland; spiritual purification is the construction of a way of life based on the ideology of a new society, having a sense of initiative and entrepreneur, selfless competition; spiritual elevation is the acquisition of a worldview based on a

Therefore, reforms in the spiritual sphere are explained by what cultural and intellectual potential the coming-of-age generation depends on. The restoration, purification and development of such spiritual values, in turn, also lead to the formation of both delightful (aesthetic) aspects in the human psyche. As a result of the combination of moral and educational qualities, aesthetic taste, pleasure culture are formed and develop.

Youth education is a continuous and regularly organized social process and should be the only system of education of the Family, School, neighborhood, higher education and community so that they do not fall under the influence of foreign worldview and destructive ideas, religious extremist groups. Such unity does not allow the destructive ideas of fanatics and extremists to spread among young people.

Raising and educating a physically healthy, morally pure, spiritually rich generation is the most pressing issue within social tasks. Literature and art occupy a special place among the means of education in the upbringing of such a generation.

The years of independence marked a change in the law of literature and art, on the one hand, the figurative appropriation of the world. Literature and art began to express the events of national life without ideological repression; on the second hand, the possibilities of influencing the consciousness and consciousness of the people expanded.

In literature and art, the principle of the commonality of social responsibility with creative freedom has been decided.

The President's decrees on the granting of the status of the state language to the Uzbek language and the celebration of this day, the establishment of the Community Center "spirituality and enlightenment", the establishment of the folk practical and decorative arts, musical education and Variety, the establishment of the Academy of Arts, the development of national dance and choreography, the establishment of the

National Art Not only aesthetically educates the youth of the nation, exalting in them feelings of patriotism, nobility, but also strengthening friendly and spiritual relations between the peoples of the world.

The five initiatives are a social phenomenon that heals the hearts of young people, forms their moral image, is one of the main factors in maturing as a spiritually perfect person.

Hence, five initiatives are humanizing, bemisl educational significance in the realization of each person's own talents and potential and in connecting the feelings of initiative, enthusiasm, creativity in them with the pleasure reality. On this basis, the young generation of Uzbekistan, whose future is great, will be brought up and their aesthetic thinking will be improved.

Today's globalization conditions demand that the aesthetic culture of the individual be perfect and Lush in every way. This is due to the fact that the changes taking place in society do not directly give anyone a chance to deviate from globalization, but those who say that I avoid it are more and more caught in his net. A person's passion for information, aesthetic tastes and experiences are leading to this situation without worrying about it.

Each individual creates in the context of globalization a delightful relationship of social progress through his spiritual maturation and aesthetic culture. At the time of this delightful relationship, such as deep assimilation and awareness of the long-standing values of our people, emotional and delightful perception of reality, thoughtful observation of the national and universal characteristics of our history become an urgent problem. Their solution, on the other hand, continues to develop in the highest spiritual-moral and artistic-aesthetic views of the individual.

Ensuring that globalization in the field of information is aimed at protecting an individual's interests is an urgent problem of our society. But it should be embodied in our activities to comprehend in all respects the processes affecting the worldview and spiritual education of the individual, to seek the mechanisms of effective functioning of factors in the development of aesthetic culture, to introduce into society the age-old values and mentality that can fight against the destructive views of various ideas and ideologies.

LIST OF USED LITERATURE

1. The Constitution of the Republic of Uzbekistan. - T.: Uzbekistan, 2018.
2. Mirziyoyev Sh.M. The law ensures stability and human dignity, the development of yurts and an abundance of people. - T.: Uzbekistan, 2017.
3. Mirziyoyev Sh.M. Our great kelazhag is kuramiz along with our man and noble khalk. - T.: Uzbekistan, 2017.
4. Mirziyoyev Sh. Since we have witnessed this event, we have witnessed how we have witnessed how we have witnessed how we have witnessed this.: Uzbekistan, 1st ed., 2018.
5. Mirziyoyev Sh.M. The highest assessment given to our activities is the agrees of our Khalk. - T.: Uzbekistan, 2nd Ed., 2018.
6. Mirziyoyev Sh.M. The Quran says that life in heaven and hell is an abundance of benefits and pleasures. - T.: Uzbekistan, 2019.
7. Karimov.A. In memory of him. - T. Vostok, 1998.
8. Karimovi.A. Highmaskuch is a language. - T.: "Spirituality", 2008.
9. Abdullaev M. Esthetician of culture:

theoretical-methodologist zhikhats. - T.: Science, 2007.

10. Abdullah Sher. The Moralist. - T.: The Young Age of Generation, 2003.

11. Avloni A. Turkish Gulistan or morality. - T.: Youth publishing house, 2018.

12. Ahmed Yassawi. The wise man.Slave to the naming of literature and publishing art. - T.: 1990.

13. Bakhronov J. The national person has English legitimacy. "Zarafshan", Samarkand-1995.

14. Boboev H., Dostzhonov T., Khasanov S. "Avesta" is an invalid Oriental folk memorial plaque. - T.: 2004.

15. The creator of the idea. - T.: Izhad Danube, 2002.

16. Gaibullaev O. Aesthetics.Educational-methodological qualification. - Samarkand: SamDCHTI, 2019.

17. Gaibullayev O. History and theory of national idea. - T.: Science and technology, 2019.

18. Gafarli M.G., A. Kasaev.Ch. the development of the Uzbek model: peace and restoration - the basis of development. - T.: Uzbekistan, 2001.

19. Gulmetov E. Globalashov heat and spiritual value // national idea and spiritual value: theory, methodology, practice. - T.: 2004.

20. Jabborov. High culture and unworthy spirituality are masked. - T.: Uzbekistan, 2012.

21. Juraev T., Akobirov S. At the same time, as in the case of other types of weapons, in the case of other types of weapons such as weapons, weapons, weapons, weapons, weapons, etc. - T.: Academia, 2007.

22. Ziemukhammadov B. Complete the book. - T.: Turan-Iqbal, 2006.

23. Ibrahim Karimov. The Glorious Nation. - T.: Young Ages, 2005.

24. Culturally significant. - T.:2006.

25. Sh. Madaeva.Yes. National mentality and democratic thinking. - T.: Philosophy and Law Publishing Institute, 2007.

26. Mamashokirov S., Togaev S. In this verse, Allah Almighty revealed that people who do not believe in him and do not obey his Messenger, peace and blessings of Allah be upon him, do not believe in him and do not obey his Messenger. - T.: Spirituality, 2007.

27. S. Mamashokirov, A. Utamurodov. The goal has been achieved. - T.: Editor, 2008.

28. Mahmudova G. Jadism and Turkish ethics-aesthetic development of thought. - T.: PERIODPRESS, 2006.

29. National idea of independence: Foundation concept and principle. - T.: Young Centuries, 2001.

30. National sovereignty of ideas and initiatives leader. - T.: Academia, 2007.

31. This is the true meaning and purpose of religion. - T.: Academy of Publishing, National Philosophical Publishing House of Uzbekistan, 2005.

32. Musaev F. Philosophy of the democratic state of Kurish-the foundations of law. - T.: Uzbekistan, 2007.

33. There are verses in the Quran indicative that the Prophet (peace and blessings of Allaah be upon him) was an imam and caliph.- T. Vostok, 1998.

34. Nizamidov N. Ancient China tarikhs, religious beliefs and culture. - T.: Science and technology, 2014.

35. Nizamiddinov N. Ancient India tarikhs, religious beliefs and culture. - T.: Science and technology, 2014.

36. Normatov K., Kyrgyzbaev A. Tashkent

city. - T.: 2007.

37. Otamuratov S. Globalization and nationality. - T.: The Young Age of Generation, 2008.

38. Otamurodov S. Yeshlar plays an important role in the development of political culture. - T.: Uzbekistan, 2015.

39. Rumi Zh. Drink. - T.: The Young age of generation, 2013.

40. Spirkin A.G. Philosophy. –M.: 2000.

41. E.Umarov, M.Abdulaev. Basic spirituality. - T. Vastok, 2005.

42. UmarovE., KarimovR., MirsaidovaM., Oykhojayevag. Estetikaasos. - T.: Chulpan, 2006.

43. Umar Hayem. Ruboils. - T.: 1991.

44. Utkin A.I. Globalization: process and understanding. – M.: Logos, 2002.

45. Fayziev S., Normatov K. Terrorism and heresy: a riddle, heresy. - T.: Philosophy and Law Publishing Institute, 2007

46. Philosophy is a section of the dictionary. - T.Vastok, 2004.

47. Basic philosophy. - T.: Uzbekistan, 2005.

48. Khasanboeva., Khasanboev J., Khamidov H. Pedagogy of tarikhi. - T.: F.In

2004, the publishing house of fulom namidagh Publishing yayaty.

49. Honazarov K. Worldview and philosophy. - T.: Philosophy and Law Institute, 2009.

50. T. Khuzhanova.J. Ideological prevention is a factor in protecting the ideas of descendants (socio-philosophical analysis). - T.: National Philosophical Society of Uzbekistan, 2019.

51. Sher A., Khusanov B., Umarov E. Aesthetics. - T.: 2008.

52. Sher A. Aesthetics.- T.: Uzbekistan, 2014.

53. Joseph's life (may Allah be pleased with him) was rich and eventful. - T.: Uzbekistan, 2006.

54. Kashkadarya militarism: traditional and modern. - T.: "The young ages of generation", 2007.

55. Kirgizbaev M. Fukara Society: Genesis, formation and development. - T.: Uzbekistan, 2005.

56. Diary. - T.: The reviewer, 2006.

57. Glorious Quran. The meaning of interpretation and interpretation. Translation and

interpretation by Sheikh Abdulaziz Mansour. - Tashkent:" Tashkent Islamic University " Association Printing press Publishing house, 2018.

58. Kusiev T. Godlessness and civilization. - T.: Culture, 2000.

59. Philosophy. - T.Vastok, 2004.

60. Yahshilikov Zh.Ya., Mukhammadiev N.E. National idea: development strategy of Uzbekistan. - T.: Chulpon, 2018.

www.ingramcontent.com/pod-product-compliance
Lightning Source LLC
LaVergne TN
LVHW010313070526
838199LV00065B/5541